DINNER

with Kids

don't cook twice, it's alright

MURDOCH BOOKS

We all adore our children but we don't always love their eating habits. To keep the peace at dinner many families resort to eating bland, kid-friendly food, or frazzled parents end up cooking two meals: one for them and one for the kids. Now help is at hand. The deliciously flexible dishes in this book are designed to keep the whole family happy. Many recipes allow the grown-ups to add a special something to jazz up their meals after the little ones have been served, so all those items that kids can't or won't eat (olives, anchovies, capers, chilli) are suddenly back on the menu. Just follow the 'for the kids' and 'for the adults' directions, then sit back and enjoy not just the fabulous meal but the harmonious vibe at the table too.

Contents

Stovetop

Lamb 'sausages' with zucchini and pea risoni • Beef goulash with dumplings • Lamb chops with sweet potato mash and chermoula • Meal-in-a-bowl soup with Gorgonzola toasts • Rice noodle, beef and vegetable stir-fry • Lamb meatballs with couscous • Mushroom and chicken risotto with olive and herb sprinkle • Turkish steak sandwich with red onion jam • Parmesan-crumbed veal with mixed vegetable mash • Beef and noodle salad with sesame dressing • Pork skewers with pineapple noodle toss • Rigatoni with sausage and tomato sugo • Cajun chicken with corn fritters and a tangy tomato relish • Braised lamb with artichoke, prosciutto and olives • Cumin-dusted chicken with corn, bean and avocado salad • Pot roast with figs, potatoes, silverbeet and skordalia • Sesame plum drumsticks with brown rice and stir-fried greens • Barbecued pork chow mein with crispy noodles • Chicken, bacon and avocado burger with mustard mayo • Pumpkin, lentil and tomato soup with cheesy toasts • Mild chilli pork with polenta and avocado salsa • Bacon, pea and walnut spaghetti carbonara • Chimichurri steak with red rice and beans • Chicken satay with peanut sauce and bok choy • Pork and ricotta rissoles with risoni and braised fennel • Chicken san choy bau • Noodle soup with fish and prawn dumplings • Lamb and lentil bolognese with wholemeal spaghetti • Braised beef with honey parsnip mash • Fish tortillas with a mango and green chilli salsa • Classic chicken noodle soup • Thai pork burgers with nahm jim salad • Teriyaki salmon with pumpkin mash and snow peas

Preparation time: 20 minutes
plus 10 minutes chilling time

Cooking time:
20 minutes

Serves:
2 adults, 2 kids

Lamb 'sausages' with zucchini and pea risoni

2 tablespoons olive oil
1 onion, finely chopped
1 garlic clove, crushed
1 teaspoon dried oregano
400 g (14 oz) minced (ground) lamb
1 egg, lightly beaten
2 tablespoons chopped flat-leaf
  (Italian) parsley
1 tablespoon chopped mint
2 tablespoons lemon juice

Minted yoghurt

250 g (9 oz/1 cup) Greek-style yoghurt
1–2 tablespoons chopped mint

Zucchini and pea risoni

200 g (7 oz/1 cup) risoni
  (rice-shaped pasta)
60 ml (2 fl oz/¼ cup) olive oil
155 g (5½ oz/1 cup) frozen peas
3 small zucchini (courgettes),
  finely sliced
10 cherry tomatoes, halved
2 tablespoons chopped flat-leaf
  (Italian) parsley
juice and finely grated rind of 1 lemon

Extras, for adults

75 g (2½ oz/½ cup) crumbled soft
  feta cheese

Heat 1 tablespoon of the olive oil in a non-stick frying pan over medium heat. Add the onion and garlic and cook for 3 minutes, or until the onion has softened. Stir in the oregano, remove from the heat and leave to cool.

Transfer the onion mixture to a large bowl. Add the lamb, egg, parsley, mint and lemon juice and mix until well combined. Divide the mixture into eight even portions, then form each into a 'sausage' about 10 cm (4 inches) long. Place on a plate, cover with plastic wrap and refrigerate for 10 minutes.

To make the minted yoghurt, put the yoghurt in a small bowl, mix the mint through, then cover and refrigerate until required.

Heat the remaining olive oil in a non-stick frying pan over medium heat. Cook the sausages for 5–6 minutes on each side, or until cooked through and browned all over.

Meanwhile, make the zucchini and pea risoni. Bring a large saucepan of salted water to the boil, add the risoni and cook according to the packet instructions, then drain well. Heat the olive oil in a large saucepan over medium heat, add the peas, zucchini and tomato and cook for 2 minutes, or until the tomato starts to soften. Stir in the risoni, parsley, lemon juice and lemon rind, then cook for 1 minute to heat through.

Serve the sausages on a bed of risoni, with a dollop of the yoghurt.

For the adults, scatter the feta over the top.

Beef goulash with dumplings

1 kg (2 lb 4 oz) beef chuck steak,
  or other stewing steak, cut into 3 cm
  (1¼ inch) cubes
1 tablespoon plain (all-purpose) flour
20 g (¾ oz) butter
2 tablespoons vegetable oil
2 onions, sliced
1 large red capsicum (pepper),
  finely chopped
2 garlic cloves, chopped
1 tablespoon sweet paprika
1 teaspoon caraway seeds
1 teaspoon thyme
1 litre (35 fl oz/4 cups) beef stock
2 tablespoons tomato paste
  (concentrated purée)
300 g (10½ oz) green beans

Dumplings
150 g (5½ oz/1 cup) self-raising flour
a large pinch of salt
30 g (1 oz) butter, melted
90 ml (3 fl oz) milk
1 tablespoon chopped flat-leaf
  (Italian) parsley

Put the beef and flour in a bowl and toss to coat the beef in the flour. Season with sea salt and freshly ground black pepper.

Heat the butter and oil in a large flameproof casserole dish. Add the beef in batches and cook, turning often, for 5–6 minutes each batch, or until browned all over. Transfer each batch to a bowl while browning the remaining beef.

Add the onion, capsicum and garlic to the casserole dish and sauté over medium heat for 5–6 minutes, or until softened. Add the paprika, caraway seeds and thyme and stir for 1 minute, then return the beef to the pan. Add the stock and tomato paste, bring to the boil over medium heat, then reduce the heat to low. Cover and cook, stirring occasionally, for 1–1½ hours, or until the beef is tender.

Meanwhile, make the dumplings. Sift the flour and salt into a large bowl and make a well in the centre. Add the melted butter, milk and parsley to the well and stir until a dough forms. Divide the dough into eight even portions and roll each into a ball.

Remove the lid from the goulash, place the dumplings on top of the beef in a single layer, then cover and simmer for 15 minutes, or until the dumplings are cooked through. (Avoid lifting the lid during this time as the dumplings need to steam to cook through properly.)

While the dumplings are cooking, bring a saucepan of salted water to the boil. Add the beans and cook for 6 minutes, or until just tender. Drain well and serve immediately, with the goulash and dumplings.

| ☀ **Preparation time:** 20 minutes | ☀ **Cooking time:** about 2 hours | ☀ **Serves:** 2 adults, 2–3 kids |

Preparation time: 20 minutes

Cooking time: 15 minutes

Serves: 2 adults, 2–3 kids

Lamb chops with sweet potato mash and chermoula

3 orange sweet potatoes (about
  1 kg/2 lb 4 oz), peeled and cut into
  2 cm (¾ inch) chunks
50 g (1¾ oz) butter, chopped
60 ml (2 fl oz/¼ cup) extra virgin
  olive oil, plus extra, for brushing
8 lamb chump chops
2 tablespoons lemon juice
2 teaspoons honey, or to taste
2 large handfuls of baby English
  spinach

Chermoula, for adults
2 teaspoons sweet paprika
2 teaspoons ground coriander
2 teaspoons ground cumin
2 tablespoons lemon juice
3 garlic cloves, finely chopped
1 tablespoon honey
1 tablespoon olive oil
1 small handful of flat-leaf (Italian)
  parsley, chopped
1 small handful of coriander (cilantro)
  leaves, chopped

To make the chermoula, put the paprika, ground coriander and cumin, lemon juice, garlic, honey and olive oil in a small bowl. Season to taste with sea salt and freshly ground pepper, mix well and set aside.

Bring a large saucepan of salted water to the boil. Add the sweet potato and cook over medium heat for 10 minutes, or until soft. Drain well, then place in a food processor with the butter and blend to a smooth purée. Season to taste with sea salt and freshly ground pepper, then transfer to a heatproof bowl. Cover with foil and keep warm.

Meanwhile, heat a chargrill pan or heavy-based frying pan to medium–high. Brush lightly with oil, add the chops and cook for 3–4 minutes on each side, or until they are done to your liking.

In a small bowl, whisk together the lemon juice, olive oil and honey, then season to taste. Divide the spinach leaves among the serving plates and drizzle the dressing over.

Divide the sweet potato mash and chops among the plates.

For the adults, mix the parsley and coriander into the chermoula and spoon it over the chops and mash.

Meal-in-a-bowl soup with Gorgonzola toasts

2 tablespoons vegetable oil
1 onion, cut into 2 cm (¾ inch) chunks
1 leek, white part only, cut into 2 cm
  (¾ inch) chunks
1 carrot, thickly sliced
1 fresh bay leaf
1.25 litres (44 fl oz/5 cups) vegetable or
  chicken stock
400 g (14 oz) tin chopped tomatoes
2 tablespoons tomato paste
  (concentrated purée)
110 g (3¾ oz/½ cup) pearl barley
¼ white cabbage (about 300 g/10½ oz),
  core removed, then cut into 2 cm
  (¾ inch) chunks
400 g (14 oz) tin borlotti (cranberry)
  beans, rinsed and drained
1 small handful of chopped basil
  (optional)

Gorgonzola toasts, for adults
4 slices of ciabatta or other rustic bread
100 g (3½ oz) Gorgonzola cheese,
  crumbled

Heat the oil in a large heavy-based saucepan over medium heat. Add the onion, leek and carrot and sauté for 5 minutes, or until softened.

Stir in the bay leaf, stock, tomatoes, tomato paste, barley and cabbage. Bring to the boil, then reduce the heat to medium–low. Cover and simmer for 1 hour, or until the vegetables and barley are tender. Season to taste with sea salt and freshly ground black pepper and stir in the borlotti beans. Bring back to a simmer, then reduce the heat to low, cover and keep warm.

Meanwhile, make the Gorgonzola toasts. Heat the grill (broiler) to medium, then put the bread slices on a baking tray and cook under the grill for 2 minutes on each side, or until golden. Sprinkle the Gorgonzola over the toasts and grill (broil) until the cheese has melted.

Ladle the soup into bowls and sprinkle with the basil, if using.

For the adults, serve the soup with the hot Gorgonzola toasts.

Preparation time:
25 minutes

Cooking time:
1 hour 15 minutes

Serves:
2 adults, 2 kids

| **Preparation time:** 15 minutes | **Cooking time:** 10 minutes | **Serves:** 2 adults, 2 kids |

Rice noodle, beef and vegetable stir-fry

150 g (5½ oz) rump or skirt steak,
   trimmed and finely sliced (*see tip*)
2 teaspoons cornflour (cornstarch)
2 teaspoons oyster sauce
1½ tablespoons soy sauce
1 garlic clove, chopped
2 tablespoons vegetable oil
1 carrot, cut into matchsticks
1 small red capsicum (pepper), sliced
3 baby bok choy (pak choy), sliced into
   2.5 cm (1 inch) chunks
500 g (1 lb 2 oz) fresh rice noodles
   (available from the Asian section in
   supermarkets or Asian food stores)
100 g (3½ oz/1 cup) bean sprouts,
   tails trimmed

Extras, for adults
chopped red chilli, to serve
coriander (cilantro) leaves, to serve

Put the steak in a bowl with the cornflour, oyster sauce, 1 teaspoon of the soy sauce and the garlic. Stir to coat well.

In a wok or large non-stick frying pan, heat 1 tablespoon of the oil over medium–high heat. Stir-fry the meat for 1–2 minutes, or until golden and cooked through. Remove from the wok and set aside.

Wipe the wok clean, then heat the remaining oil over medium–high heat. Add the carrot and capsicum and cook for 1–2 minutes, then add the bok choy and cook for another minute, or until it begins to wilt. Add the noodles, beef mixture and remaining soy sauce and cook, tossing, for 5–6 minutes, or until the noodles soften and the ingredients are well combined.

Toss the bean sprouts through, then remove from the heat and leave to stand for 1–2 minutes. Remove the children's portions and serve.

For the adults, serve the noodles sprinkled with chilli and coriander.

It will be easier to slice the beef thinly if you partially freeze it first.

Lamb meatballs with couscous

1 tablespoon vegetable oil
½ large onion, finely chopped
1 garlic clove, crushed
½ teaspoon ground cumin
¾ teaspoon ground cinnamon
a pinch of saffron
2 tablespoons honey
125 g (4½ oz/⅔ cup) pitted
  dates, chopped
2 tablespoons tomato paste
  (concentrated purée)
400 g (14 oz) tin chopped tomatoes
375 g (13 oz/2 cups) instant couscous
20 g (¾ oz) butter
1 tablespoon olive oil

Lamb meatballs

500 g (1 lb 2 oz) minced (ground) lamb
½ large onion, finely diced
1 garlic clove, crushed
1 tablespoon fennel seeds
½ teaspoon ground cumin
¼ teaspoon ground cinnamon
2 tablespoons tomato paste
  (concentrated purée)
1 small handful of coriander (cilantro)
  leaves, chopped
1 small handful of chopped flat-leaf
  (Italian) parsley

Extras, for adults

chopped coriander (cilantro) leaves,
  to serve

Put all the ingredients for the lamb meatballs in a bowl. Season with sea salt and freshly ground black pepper and mix together well. Take heaped teaspoons of the mixture and roll them into little balls, then set aside.

Heat the vegetable oil in a flameproof casserole dish or a large frying pan over medium heat. Add the onion and garlic and sauté for 2 minutes. Stir in the cumin, cinnamon, saffron, honey, dates, tomato paste and tomatoes and bring to a simmer, then cook over medium–low heat for 5 minutes.

Gently place the meatballs in the tomato sauce, then cover and cook over low heat for 30 minutes, or until the meatballs are firm and cooked through, stirring occasionally.

Meanwhile, put the couscous in a heatproof bowl and pour 500 ml (17 fl oz/2 cups) boiling water over. Add the butter and olive oil, season well, then fluff up the grains with a fork. Cover with plastic wrap and leave to stand for 5 minutes, then fluff up the grains with a fork again to break up any lumps.

Divide the couscous among shallow bowls, top with the meatballs and serve to the kids.

For the adults, serve sprinkled with coriander.

Preparation time:
30 minutes

Cooking time:
40 minutes

Serves:
2 adults, 2 kids

Preparation time:
20 minutes

Cooking time:
40 minutes

Serves:
2 adults, 2 kids

Mushroom and chicken risotto with olive and herb sprinkle

1.125 litres (40 fl oz/4½ cups) chicken stock
1 tablespoon olive oil
20 g (¾ oz) butter
2 leeks, white part only, finely sliced
1 garlic clove, crushed
400 g (14 oz/4½ cups) sliced Swiss brown mushrooms (*see tip*)
330 g (11½ oz/1½ cups) arborio rice
2 small chicken breasts fillets (about 350 g/12 oz), diced
1 large handful of baby English spinach leaves
65 g (2¼ oz/⅔ cup) finely grated parmesan cheese

Olive and herb sprinkle, for adults
110 g (3¾ oz/½ cup) green olives, pitted and finely sliced
1 small handful of basil, torn
1 small handful of flat-leaf (Italian) parsley, torn
1 tablespoon grated lemon rind

Extras, for adults
25 g (1 oz/¼ cup) shaved parmesan cheese

Put all the ingredients for the olive and herb sprinkle in a small bowl. Mix together and set aside until ready to serve.

Bring the stock to the boil in a saucepan, then keep hot over low heat.

Heat the olive oil and butter in a large heavy-based saucepan over medium heat. Add the leek and garlic and sauté for 2 minutes, or until the leek has softened. Add the mushrooms and cook for a further 2 minutes, or until softened.

Add the rice and stir using a wooden spoon until the grains are well coated. Add a ladleful of hot stock to the rice and stir until the liquid has been completely absorbed. Continue to add the stock, one ladleful at a time, stirring constantly until the rice absorbs the stock before adding more. Stir in the chicken with the last ladlefuls of stock and cook for 5 minutes, or until the rice is al dente and creamy and the chicken is cooked through.

Stir in the spinach and parmesan and divide among serving bowls.

For the adults, serve scattered with shaved parmesan and the olive and herb sprinkle.

Instead of the Swiss brown mushrooms you can use a mixture of mushrooms (such as oyster and fresh shiitake) if you prefer.

Turkish steak sandwich with red onion jam

Instead of making the red onion jam, you could simply use a good relish or chutney. Chargrilled lamb backstraps or loin fillets are also delicious here instead of minute steaks. Slice them thinly on the diagonal before cooking.

olive oil, for brushing
1 loaf of Turkish bread, cut into 4 even
   portions
4 x 80–100 g (2¾–3½ oz) pieces of
   minute (thin) steak, pounded thinly
   using a meat mallet
hummus, to serve
225 g (8 oz) tin sliced beetroot (beets),
   drained
3 large tomatoes, sliced
1 large handful of shredded iceberg
   lettuce
mayonnaise, to drizzle

Red onion jam, for adults
1 tablespoon olive oil
1 large red onion, halved and
   finely sliced
1 garlic clove, finely chopped
1 tablespoon soft brown sugar
1 tablespoon balsamic vinegar

Extras, for adults
3 Japanese (slender) eggplants
   (aubergines), cut into slices 5 mm
   (¼ inch) thick
2 zucchini (courgettes), cut lengthways
   into slices 5 mm (¼ inch) thick

To make the red onion jam, heat the olive oil in a saucepan, add the onion and garlic and cook over low heat, stirring often, for 10–12 minutes, or until the onion is very soft and deep golden. Add the sugar, vinegar and 2 tablespoons water and cook for a further 10–12 minutes, or until thick and jammy.

Meanwhile to make the extras **for the adults**, preheat a chargrill pan or large frying pan to medium. Lightly brush the eggplant and zucchini slices with olive oil, then cook in batches for 2–3 minutes on each side, or until tender. Set aside in a bowl, reserving the pan.

Preheat the grill (broiler) to medium. Cut the Turkish bread into four even portions, then slice each in half lengthways. Place on a baking tray and lightly toast both sides under the grill.

Lightly brush the steaks with olive oil and chargrill over medium heat for 1–2 minutes on each side, or until done to your liking.

Spread half the Turkish bread bases with hummus, then add the beetroot.

For the adults, add the eggplant and zucchini.

Top all the sandwiches with the steak, tomato slices and some lettuce, then drizzle with mayonnaise. Place the other bread slices on top and cut each sandwich in half (or into quarters for the kids).

For the adults, serve with the onion jam.

✳ Preparation time:	✳ Cooking time:	✳ Serves:
30 minutes	30 minutes	2 adults, 2 kids

| ✳ **Preparation time:** 25 minutes | ✳ **Cooking time:** 20 minutes | ✳ **Serves:** 2 adults, 2–3 kids |

Parmesan-crumbed veal with mixed vegetable mash

160 g (5¾ oz/2 cups) fresh white
  breadcrumbs
50 g (1¾ oz/½ cup) finely grated
  parmesan cheese
75 g (2½ oz/½ cup) plain
  (all-purpose) flour
2 eggs
1 garlic clove, crushed
6 thin slices of veal (about 350 g/
  12 oz in total), pounded very thinly
  using a meat mallet
20 g (¾ oz) butter
2 tablespoons olive oil
lemon wedges, to serve

Mixed vegetable mash
500 g (1 lb 2 oz) butternut pumpkin
  (winter squash), peeled and chopped
2 potatoes, peeled and chopped
155 g (5½ oz/1 cup) frozen peas
20 g (¾ oz) butter
60 ml (2 fl oz/¼ cup) warm milk

To make the mixed vegetable mash, bring a saucepan of lightly salted water to the boil, add the pumpkin and potato and cook for 10–15 minutes, or until nearly tender. Add the peas and cook for 1 minute. Drain well, then return the vegetables to the saucepan. Add the butter and milk, season to taste with sea salt and freshly ground black pepper and mash lightly. Cover and keep warm.

In a large bowl, mix together the breadcrumbs and parmesan. Put the flour in a large bowl and season well. Break the eggs into another bowl and whisk with the garlic.

Dip each slice of veal into the flour, shaking off the excess. Working with one piece of veal at a time, dip each slice into the egg mixture, allowing the excess to drain off, then dip into the breadcrumb mixture, pressing the crumbs firmly on both sides to coat well.

Meanwhile, heat half the butter and half the olive oil in a large, heavy-based frying pan over medium heat. Gently lay half the veal slices in the pan and cook for 1–1½ minutes on each side, or until the crumbs are golden and the veal is cooked through. Keep warm and repeat with the remaining oil, butter and veal.

Serve immediately, with the mash and lemon wedges.

Beef and noodle salad with sesame dressing

To make the noodles easier to eat, cut them into shorter lengths using a clean, sharp pair of scissors. To toast sesame seeds, put them in a frying pan over medium–low heat and briefly fry until they brown and turn fragrant, shaking the pan so they toast evenly and don't burn.

225 g (8 oz) dried egg noodles
  (*see tip*)
250 g (9 oz) rump steak, trimmed
  and finely sliced
1 tablespoon soy sauce
3 teaspoons cornflour (cornstarch)
1 tablespoon peanut oil
140 g (5 oz/1½ cups) bean sprouts,
  tails trimmed
1 Lebanese (short) cucumber, halved,
  then finely sliced on the diagonal
1 carrot, cut into thin matchsticks
2 tablespoons sesame seeds, toasted
  (*see tip*)

Sesame dressing

2 tablespoons Chinese sesame paste
  (available from Asian supermarkets,
  or substitute with tahini)
2 tablespoons light soy sauce
2 teaspoons caster (superfine) sugar
1½ teaspoons rice wine vinegar
1 teaspoon sesame oil

Extras, for adults

1 large handful of coriander (cilantro)
  leaves
1 small red chilli, chopped

Bring a large saucepan of water to the boil. Add the egg noodles and cook for 4 minutes, or according to the packet instructions. Drain the noodles, then rinse under cold running water and drain again. Place in a large bowl.

Put the beef, soy sauce and cornflour in a bowl and mix well. Heat the peanut oil in a wok or large non-stick frying pan over medium–high heat. Add the beef mixture and stir-fry for 2–3 minutes, or until the beef is cooked and golden brown. Add to the noodles with the bean sprouts, cucumber, carrot and sesame seeds.

Put all the sesame dressing ingredients in a small bowl with 2–3 tablespoons warm water. Whisk until smooth, then drizzle over the noodle salad and toss to mix well.

For the kids, remove a third of the noodle salad and serve.

For the adults, toss the coriander leaves and chilli through the rest of the noodle salad before serving.

✳ **Preparation time:**	✳ **Cooking time:**	✳ **Serves:**
20 minutes	10 minutes	2 adults, 2 kids

| ✳ **Preparation time:** 30 minutes
plus 30 minutes soaking and marinating | ✳ **Cooking time:**
20 minutes | ✳ **Serves:**
2 adults, 2 kids |

Pork skewers with pineapple noodle toss

600 g (1 lb 5 oz) pork loin steaks,
  or pork fillet, trimmed and cut into
  2 cm (¾ inch) chunks
1 tablespoon fish sauce
1 garlic clove, crushed
2 teaspoons grated fresh ginger
1 tablespoon soft brown sugar
lime wedges, to serve

Pineapple noodle toss
150 g (5½ oz) rice vermicelli
1 tablespoon vegetable oil
1 carrot, cut into matchsticks
12 snow peas (mangetout), trimmed
  and sliced lengthways
220 g (7¾ oz) tin pineapple pieces,
  drained
1½ tablespoons fish sauce
90 g (3¼ oz/1 cup) bean sprouts,
  tails trimmed

Extras, for adults
2 tablespoons toasted peanuts,
  chopped
1 bird's eye chilli, sliced
1 small handful of chopped coriander
  (cilantro) leaves
1 tablespoon lime juice
1½ tablespoons fish sauce
1 tablespoon soft brown sugar

Soak 12 wooden skewers in cold water for 30 minutes to prevent scorching.

Put the pork in a bowl with the fish sauce, garlic, ginger and sugar. Toss to coat the pork well, then cover and refrigerate for 30 minutes. Drain the pork well, then thread about four pieces onto each skewer.

Meanwhile, put the noodles in a heatproof bowl and pour enough boiling water over to just cover. Leave to stand for 10 minutes, or until softened. Drain well.

To cook the pork skewers, heat a lightly oiled chargrill pan or frying pan to medium–high. Cook the pork for 3–4 minutes on each side, or until golden and cooked to your liking. Keep warm.

Meanwhile, prepare the pineapple noodle toss. Heat the oil in a large frying pan or wok over medium heat. Add the carrot and snow peas and stir-fry for 1 minute, then add the noodles, pineapple and fish sauce and stir-fry for another 1–2 minutes. Toss the bean sprouts through, then remove about a third of the noodle mixture for the children and keep warm.

For the adults, toss the peanuts, chilli, coriander, lime juice, fish sauce and sugar through the remaining noodles and cook for a further minute, or until fragrant.

Divide the noodle toss among serving plates, top with the pork skewers and serve immediately, with lime wedges.

Rigatoni with sausage and tomato sugo

300 g (10½ oz) good-quality Italian
  sausages, casings removed
1 onion, finely chopped
1 carrot, finely chopped
400 g (14 oz) tin chopped tomatoes
2 garlic cloves, crushed
400 g (14 oz) rigatoni

Extras, for adults
1 handful of rocket (arugula), roughly
  chopped
2 tablespoons ligurian or other small
  black olives
shaved parmesan cheese, to serve

Heat a non-stick frying pan over medium–high heat. Add the sausages and cook for about 5 minutes, breaking them up with a wooden spoon to crumble the meat. Add the onion and carrot and sauté for 5 minutes, or until softened. Stir in the tomatoes and garlic and reduce the heat to medium. Cook for a further 8–10 minutes, or until the vegetables are tender and the mixture has thickened.

Meanwhile, bring a large saucepan of salted water to the boil. Add the pasta and cook according to the packet instructions. Drain, reserving about 125 ml (4 fl oz/½ cup) of the cooking water.

Stir the drained pasta into the sauce, adding some of the reserved cooking water to thin the sauce slightly if necessary. Season with sea salt and freshly ground black pepper, then transfer the children's portions to serving bowls and serve.

For the adults, stir the rocket and olives into the remaining pasta mixture until the leaves just wilt. Spoon into serving bowls, scatter with parmesan shavings and serve.

✳ Preparation time:	✳ Cooking time:	✳ Serves:
15 minutes	20 minutes	2 adults, 2 kids

Preparation time:
25 minutes

Cooking time:
35 minutes

Serves:
2 adults, 2–3 kids

Cajun chicken with corn fritters and a tangy tomato relish

vegetable oil, for pan-frying
6 chicken thighs fillets
    (about 500 g/1 lb 2 oz in total),
    trimmed, then cut in half lengthways
1 tablespoon cajun seasoning (available
    from supermarkets)
1 lime, cut into wedges

Tangy tomato relish
1 tablespoon olive oil
1 small red onion, finely chopped
1 garlic clove, crushed
1 teaspoon finely grated fresh ginger
400 g (14 oz) tin chopped tomatoes
1 tablespoon soft brown sugar
2 tablespoons fresh lime juice

Corn fritters
110 g (3¾ oz/¾ cup) plain
    (all-purpose) flour
½ teaspoon bicarbonate of soda
    (baking soda)
½ teaspoon paprika
2 eggs, lightly beaten
125 ml (4 fl oz/½ cup) milk
300 g (10½ oz/2 cups) frozen corn
    kernels, thawed and drained well
2 spring onions (scallions), finely sliced

Extras, for adults
chopped coriander (cilantro) leaves,
    to serve
1 teaspoon finely chopped red chilli

To make the tangy tomato relish, heat the olive oil in a small frying pan over medium heat and sauté the onion, garlic and ginger for 5 minutes, or until softened. Add the tomatoes, sugar and lime juice and cook over low heat for 30 minutes, or until the sauce is thick and slightly jammy.

Meanwhile, make the corn fritters. Sift the flour, bicarbonate of soda and paprika into a bowl and season well with sea salt and freshly ground black pepper. In a small bowl, whisk the eggs and milk until combined, then add to the flour mixture and whisk to a smooth batter. Stir in the corn and spring onion, then cover and leave to stand for 10 minutes.

Heat 1 tablespoon of oil over medium heat in a non-stick frying pan. Working in batches, spoon 2 tablespoons of batter per fritter into the pan, spreading it if necessary to form rounds (you should end up with about 12 fritters). Cook for 2–3 minutes on each side, or until golden and cooked through, adding extra oil to the pan as needed. Cover the fritters and keep warm.

Coat the chicken pieces with the cajun seasoning and some sea salt and freshly ground black pepper, then brush with oil.

Heat a chargrill pan or heavy-based frying pan over high heat. Cook the chicken pieces for 4 minutes on each side, or until cooked through and golden.

Divide the corn fritters among plates and top with the chicken. Spoon some of the plain tomato relish over the children's portions.

For the adults, stir the coriander and chilli through the remaining tomato relish and spoon over the chicken. Serve with lime wedges.

Braised lamb with artichoke, prosciutto and olives

2 tablespoons olive oil
1.2 kg (2 lb 12 oz) boned shoulder of lamb, trimmed and cut into 5 cm (2 inch) chunks
2 onions, chopped
2 garlic cloves, finely chopped
500 ml (17 fl oz/2 cups) chicken or vegetable stock
3 strips lemon zest, white pith removed
1½ tablespoons chopped marjoram or oregano, plus extra, for sprinkling
300 g (10½ oz) kipfler (fingerling) or other waxy potatoes, scrubbed and cut into 1 cm (½ inch) slices
3 carrots, cut into 1 cm (½ inch) slices

Extras, for adults

400 g (14 oz) tin artichoke hearts, drained and quartered
4 thin slices of prosciutto, cut into wide strips
12 kalamata olives

Heat half the olive oil in a large flameproof casserole dish over medium heat. Add the lamb in batches and cook for 2–3 minutes on each side, or until browned all over. Transfer each batch to a bowl while browning the remaining lamb.

Heat the remaining oil in the pan, then sauté the onion over low heat for 5 minutes, or until softened but not browned. Add the garlic and cook for 1 minute, then stir in the stock, lemon zest and marjoram and bring to the boil. Reduce the heat to low, return the lamb to the pan, season generously with sea salt and freshly ground black pepper and mix well. Cover and simmer over low heat for 1½ hours.

Stir in the potato and carrot. Cover and simmer for a further 40 minutes, or until the potato and meat are very tender. Skim the excess fat from the top of the braise.

Divide the braise among shallow serving bowls for the children and serve.

For the adults, add the artichoke, prosciutto and olives to the remaining braise and heat through. Serve sprinkled with marjoram, with steamed green vegetables if desired.

Preparation time:
30 minutes

Cooking time:
2 hours 30 minutes

Serves:
2 adults, 2–3 kids

| ☀ **Preparation time:** 20 minutes | ☀ **Cooking time:** 20 minutes | ☀ **Serves:** 2 adults, 2–3 kids |

Cumin-dusted chicken with corn, bean and avocado salad

55 g (2 oz/½ cup) besan (chickpea flour), available from Indian grocers and health food stores
1 teaspoon ground cumin
2 eggs
750 g (1 lb 10 oz/ about 12) chicken tenderloins, trimmed of sinew
olive oil, for pan-frying

Corn, bean and avocado salad
2 corn cobs, husks and silk removed
1 avocado, cut into thin wedges
2 tomatoes, cut into 1 cm (½ inch) chunks
400 g (14 oz) tin red kidney beans, rinsed and drained
60 ml (2 fl oz/¼ cup) extra virgin olive oil
2 tablespoons lemon juice

Extras, for adults
1 small handful of coriander (cilantro) leaves, roughly chopped
½ teaspoon Tabasco sauce, or to taste

To make the corn, bean and avocado salad, cook the corn cobs in a saucepan of boiling salted water for 8–10 minutes, or until the kernels are tender. Drain well and cool. Using a large sharp knife, remove the kernels from the cobs and place in a bowl with the avocado, tomato and beans. Whisk together the olive oil and lemon juice, season to taste with sea salt and freshly ground black pepper, then pour over the salad and toss gently to combine. Set aside.

In a bowl, mix together the besan and cumin and season with salt and pepper. Break the eggs into a bowl and lightly beat. Dust the chicken with the besan mixture, shaking off the excess, then dip each tenderloin in the beaten egg, draining off the excess. Dip them in the besan mixture again to coat well.

Heat about 1 cm (½ inch) olive oil in a large, deep frying pan over medium–high heat. Cook the chicken in two batches, frying for 2 minutes on each side, or until golden and cooked through. Drain well on paper towels.

For the kids, serve the chicken immediately with the salad.

For the adults, toss the coriander and Tabasco through the remaining salad and serve.

Any leftover chicken is delicious served cold the next day. If your children will eat parsley, stir some chopped flat-leaf (Italian) parsley into their salad before serving.

Pot roast with figs, potatoes, silverbeet and skordalia

Skordalia can be made up to 2 days ahead and stored in an airtight container in the refrigerator. Bring to room temperature before using.

2 tablespoons olive oil
1 kg (2 lb 4 oz) beef pot roast
  (topside or round)
1 small onion, finely chopped
2 carrots, thickly sliced
2 celery stalks, sliced
2 tablespoons plain (all-purpose) flour
1.125 litres (44 fl oz/4½ cups) beef stock
500 g (1 lb 2 oz) small new potatoes
125 g (4½ oz/¾ cup) dried figs, halved
3 thyme sprigs
1 kg (2 lb 4 oz/1 bunch) silverbeet
  (Swiss chard), tough stems removed,
  leaves washed and torn
2 spring onions (scallions), cut into
  2 cm (¾ inch) pieces

Skordalia, for adults

65 g (2¼ oz/¾ cup) flaked almonds
40 g (1½ oz/½ cup) fresh breadcrumbs,
  from a good, rustic-style loaf
2 large garlic cloves, chopped
1 tablespoon lemon juice, or to taste
100 ml (3½ fl oz) extra virgin olive oil

Heat half the olive oil in a large heavy-based saucepan over medium heat. Add the beef and cook, turning, for 7–8 minutes, or until browned all over. Remove to a plate and set aside.

Heat the remaining oil in the pan and sauté the onion, carrot and celery for 4 minutes, or until starting to soften. Sprinkle the flour over the top, then stir in with a wooden spoon until combined. Gradually pour in the stock, stirring constantly to prevent lumps forming.

Return the beef to the pan with the potatoes, figs and thyme sprigs. Bring to the boil, then reduce the heat to low, cover and simmer for 1 hour 20 minutes, or until the beef is tender. Remove the lid and simmer for another 15 minutes to allow the sauce to thicken. Stir in the silverbeet and cook for another 3–4 minutes, or until the silverbeet has wilted. Stir in the spring onion.

Meanwhile, make the skordalia. Put the almonds, breadcrumbs and garlic in a small food processor and blend until very finely chopped. Add the lemon juice then, with the motor running, add the olive oil in a slow, steady stream until a smooth paste forms. Add a little water to loosen the sauce, then season to taste with sea salt and freshly ground black pepper and a little extra lemon juice, if needed. Cover and set aside.

When the pot roast is cooked, remove the pan from the heat, then cover and leave to stand for 10 minutes before carving the meat. Serve slices of meat with the vegetables and sauce spooned over.

For the adults, serve with the skordalia.

| ✳ **Preparation time:** | ✳ **Cooking time:** | ✳ **Serves:** |
| 20 minutes | 2 hours | 2 adults, 2–3 kids |

Preparation time: 30 minutes
plus 1 hour marinating

Cooking time:
45 minutes

Serves:
2 adults, 3 kids

Sesame plum drumsticks with brown rice and stir-fried greens

2 tablespoons peanut or vegetable oil
150 ml (5 fl oz) chicken stock
80 ml (2½ fl oz/⅓ cup) Chinese plum
  sauce (*see tip*)
200 g (7 oz/1 cup) long-grain
  brown rice
2 tablespoons vegetable oil
300 g (10½ oz) Chinese broccoli
  (gai larn), trimmed and cut into
  3–4 cm (1¼–1½ inch) lengths
150 g (5½ oz) snow peas (mangetout),
  trimmed
2 tablespoons chicken stock or water

Sesame plum drumsticks
2 tablespoons soy sauce
1 tablespoon Chinese rice wine
  (optional; *see tip*)
1 teaspoon finely grated fresh ginger
1 teaspoon sesame oil
1 teaspoon Chinese five-spice
8 chicken drumsticks (about 1.4 kg/
  3 lb 2 oz in total), knuckle end trimmed
  (ask your butcher to do this)

Extras, for adults
1 spring onion (scallion), finely
  sliced on the diagonal
2 tablespoons sesame seeds,
  toasted

For the sesame plum drumsticks, put the soy sauce, rice wine (if using), ginger, sesame oil and five-spice in a dish large enough to hold all the drumsticks quite snugly. Cut a few diagonal slashes across each drumstick, down to the bone. Toss the drumsticks in the marinade, coating well, then cover and refrigerate for at least 1 hour.

Drain the drumsticks well, reserving the marinade. Heat the peanut oil in a wok or large non-stick frying pan over high heat. Add the drumsticks in batches and cook for 5–6 minutes, turning often until browned all over. Return all the drumsticks to the wok, pour in the stock, plum sauce and reserved marinade and bring to a simmer. Reduce the heat to low, then cook for 30 minutes, turning often, until the chicken is cooked through and the sauce is reduced and sticky.

Meanwhile, put the rice in a saucepan with 750 ml (26 fl oz/3 cups) water and bring to the boil. Cover, reduce the heat to low, then simmer for 30 minutes, or until all the water is absorbed and the rice is tender.

For the stir-fried greens, heat the vegetable oil in a wok or large non-stick frying pan over high heat. Add the Chinese broccoli and snow peas and stir-fry for 1 minute. Add the stock, then cover and cook for 2 minutes, or until the broccoli is wilted.

Serve the chicken on a bed of rice with the stir-fried greens.

For the adults, sprinkle with the spring onion and sesame seeds.

You'll find Chinese rice wine (also called shaoxing rice wine) and Chinese plum sauce in the Asian section of larger supermarkets.

Barbecued pork chow mein with crispy noodles

2 tablespoons oyster sauce
2 teaspoons soy sauce
1 teaspoon sugar
375 ml (13 fl oz/1½ cups) chicken stock
1½ tablespoons cornflour (cornstarch)
1–2 tablespoons vegetable oil
1 bunch broccolini (about 250 g/9 oz),
  chopped into 5 cm (2 inch) lengths
1 carrot, cut into thin matchsticks
150 g (5½ oz/3½ cups) shredded
  Chinese cabbage (wong bok)
175 g (6 oz/1 cup) sliced Chinese
  barbecued pork (char sui)
2 garlic cloves, chopped
1 teaspoon finely grated fresh ginger
2 spring onions (scallions), cut into
  2 cm (¾ inch) lengths
2 x 100 g (3½ oz) packets fried noodles

In a small bowl mix together the oyster sauce, soy sauce, sugar, stock and cornflour until smooth. Set aside.

Heat the oil in a wok or large non-stick frying pan over medium–high heat. Add the broccolini and carrot and stir-fry for 1 minute, or until just beginning to soften. Add the cabbage, toss for a further minute, then add the pork, garlic and ginger, tossing for another 1 minute, or until fragrant.

Stir in the soy sauce mixture, bring to the boil, then reduce the heat and simmer for 2 minutes, or until the sauce thickens. Toss the spring onion through.

Crumble the fried noodles onto a platter or serving plates, top with the chow mein and serve.

| ✳ **Preparation time:** 15–20 minutes | ✳ **Cooking time:** 10 minutes | ✳ **Serves:** 2 adults, 2 kids |

| ☀ **Preparation time:** 15 minutes | ☀ **Cooking time:** 25 minutes | ☀ **Serves:** 2 adults, 2–3 kids |

Chicken, bacon and avocado burger with mustard mayo

750 g (1 lb 10 oz) minced
  (ground) chicken
2 spring onions (scallions),
  finely sliced
125 g (4½ oz/1½ cups) fresh
  breadcrumbs
1 egg, lightly beaten
2 tablespoons chopped flat-leaf
  (Italian) parsley
1 tablespoon olive oil
6 slices of bacon, cut in half
6 hamburger buns
butter lettuce leaves, to serve
2 tomatoes, sliced
1 large avocado, sliced

Mustard mayo, for adults
125 g (4 oz/½ cup) whole-egg
  mayonnaise
3 teaspoons lemon juice
1 tablespoon wholegrain mustard,
  or to taste

Put the chicken, spring onion, breadcrumbs, egg and parsley in a bowl and season with sea salt and freshly ground black pepper. Using clean hands, mix until well combined, then divide into six even portions. Using damp hands, form each into a 12 cm (4½ inch) round, then flatten slightly to form patties.

Heat the olive oil in a large frying pan over medium heat. Cook the patties in two batches for 4 minutes on each side, or until golden and cooked through. Drain on paper towels, reserving the pan, then transfer to a plate and cover with foil to keep warm.

Wipe the pan clean, then cook the bacon for 3 minutes on each side, or until crisp. Drain on paper towels.

Meanwhile, preheat the grill (broiler) to medium. Slice the hamburger buns in half through the middle, place on a baking tray and toast under the grill on both sides until golden.

In a bowl, mix together the mustard mayo ingredients. Transfer the hamburger bases to plates, then top each with some lettuce leaves, a pattie, some tomato, bacon and avocado. Top the children's burgers with the hamburger lids and serve.

For the adults, spoon some mustard mayo over the adult burgers before putting the lids on top.

Use Turkish bread, focaccia rolls, panini or split pitta breads in place of hamburger buns if desired. In the mustard mayo you could instead use a smooth mustard such as dijon, or even horseradish cream. The uncooked burgers can be made ahead and frozen, but you'll need to completely thaw them before cooking.

Pumpkin, lentil and tomato soup with cheesy toasts

Instead of cheddar, you can top the toasts with Swiss cheese, or some gruyère cheese for adults. If you prefer a smooth soup, purée it before serving. Any leftover soup freezes well, or can be refrigerated for 3–4 days and reheated. This soup is suitable for vegetarians if made with vegetable stock.

2 tablespoons olive oil
1 kg (2 lb 4 oz) pumpkin (winter squash), peeled, seeded and cut into 2 cm (¾ inch) chunks
2 carrots, finely chopped
2 onions, finely chopped
1 large celery stalk, finely chopped
3 garlic cloves, crushed
1.5 litres (52 fl oz/6 cups) vegetable or chicken stock
125 g (4½ oz/½ cup) red lentils
400 g (14 oz) tin chopped tomatoes
1 tablespoon finely chopped parsley or coriander (cilantro) leaves

Cheesy toasts
8 slices of ciabatta or other rustic bread, cut about 2 cm (¾ inch) thick
85 g (3 oz/⅔ cup) finely grated cheddar cheese (*see tip*)

Heat the oil in a large saucepan over medium heat. Add the vegetables and garlic and sauté for 5 minutes, or until softened but not browned.

Stir in the stock, lentils and tomatoes. Bring to the boil, then reduce the heat to medium–low and simmer for 20 minutes, or until the lentils are tender. Season well with sea salt and freshly ground black pepper.

Meanwhile, make the cheesy toasts. Heat the grill (broiler) to medium, then place the bread slices on a baking tray and toast under the grill on one side. Turn the toasts over and scatter with the grated cheese. Grill for 3–4 minutes, or until the cheese has melted and is golden brown.

Ladle the soup into bowls or cups, sprinkle with parsley and serve with the hot cheesy toasts.

Preparation time:
20 minutes

Cooking time:
25 minutes

Serves:
2 adults, 2 kids

| ✳ **Preparation time:** | ✳ **Cooking time:** | ✳ **Serves:** |
| 30 minutes | 1 hour 30 minutes | 2 adults, 3 kids |

Mild chilli pork with polenta and avocado salsa

2 tablespoons vegetable oil
1 kg (2 lb 4 oz) pork shoulder, trimmed
  and cut into 1 cm (½ inch) chunks
1 onion, finely chopped
1 red capsicum (pepper), finely chopped
3 garlic cloves, crushed
½ teaspoon ground cumin
¼ teaspoon chilli powder, or to taste
  (optional)
400 g (14 oz) tin chopped tomatoes
125 ml (4 fl oz/½ cup) beef stock
125 g (4½ oz/½ cup) sour cream
½ avocado, chopped

Polenta
500 ml (17 fl oz/2 cups) milk
150 g (5½ oz/1 cup) white or yellow
  polenta
40 g (1½ oz) butter

Avocado salsa, for adults
½ avocado, chopped
1 large handful of coriander (cilantro)
  leaves, torn
1 tablespoon lime or lemon juice
1 long red chilli, sliced
a large pinch of chilli flakes (optional)

Heat 1 tablespoon of the oil in a large heavy-based saucepan over medium–high heat. Add the pork in batches and cook for 2–3 minutes on each side, or until browned all over. Transfer each batch to a bowl while browning the remaining pork.

Heat the remaining oil in the pan over medium heat and sauté the onion for 3 minutes, or until softened. Stir in the capsicum, garlic, cumin and chilli powder, if using, and cook for a further 1–2 minutes, or until aromatic. Return the pork to the pan and add the tomatoes and stock. Stir well and bring to the boil, then reduce the heat to medium–low. Cover and simmer for 1¼ hours, or until the pork is tender.

Meanwhile, make the polenta. Put the milk in a saucepan with 500 ml (17 fl oz/2 cups) water and bring to the boil. Stirring continuously, add the polenta in a thin, steady stream. Cook over low heat, stirring often, for 30–35 minutes, or until the polenta is thick and soft. Remove from the heat and stir in the butter.

To make the avocado salsa, put the avocado in a small bowl with the coriander, lime juice, chilli and chilli flakes, if using. Very gently mix together.

Put half the pork mixture in a bowl. Reserve 2 tablespoons of the sour cream, then stir the remaining sour cream through the pork. Divide the polenta among shallow serving bowls or plates.

For the kids, top the polenta with the creamy pork mixture, then the chopped avocado.

For the adults, top with the remaining pork mixture, then the avocado salsa and a dollop of the remaining sour cream.

Bacon, pea and walnut spaghetti carbonara

If you like an extra-creamy pasta, add another 125 ml (4 fl oz/½ cup) cream to the egg mixture. Chopped fresh mushrooms are another delicious addition — cook them together with the bacon.

500 g (1 lb 2 oz) spaghetti
4 slices of bacon (about 400 g/14 oz), rind and excess fat removed
1 tablespoon olive oil
3 garlic cloves, finely chopped
155 g (5½ oz/1 cup) frozen peas, thawed
4 eggs
75 g (2½ oz/¾ cup) grated parmesan cheese
185 ml (6 fl oz/¾ cup) cream

Extras, for adults
90 g (3¼ oz/¾ cup) toasted walnuts, chopped
1 tablespoon chopped flat-leaf (Italian) parsley
grated parmesan cheese, to serve

Bring a large saucepan of salted water to the boil. Add the spaghetti and cook according to the packet instructions.

Meanwhile, cut the bacon into 5 mm (¼ inch) strips. Heat the olive oil in a frying pan over medium heat, then add the bacon strips and cook for 5 minutes, or until slightly crisp. Add the garlic and peas and sauté over low heat for 3 minutes. Remove from the heat and set aside.

In a small bowl whisk together the eggs, parmesan and cream. Season to taste with sea salt and freshly ground black pepper.

When the spaghetti is al dente, drain well, then return to the pan and gently toss over low heat for 2 minutes to evaporate any liquid. Toss the bacon and peas through, then add the egg mixture. Stir for 1–2 minutes, taking care not to let the mixture boil or the eggs will scramble. Remove from the heat, cover and leave to stand for 2–3 minutes, or until the sauce thickens.

For the kids, serve the pasta in warmed bowls.

For the adults, toss the walnuts through the remaining pasta. Serve sprinkled with parsley and extra parmesan.

| ☀ **Preparation time:** 15 minutes | ☀ **Cooking time:** 20 minutes | ☀ **Serves:** 2 adults, 2–3 kids |

✳ **Preparation time:** 20 minutes
plus overnight marinating

✳ **Cooking time:**
35 minutes

✳ **Serves:**
2 adults, 2–3 kids

Chimichurri steak with red rice and beans

800 g (1 lb 12 oz) piece of skirt steak
   (about 1 cm/½ inch thick), trimmed
   of all sinew
1 bunch (150 g/5½ oz) flat-leaf (Italian)
   parsley, leaves picked
1 tablespoon dried oregano
60 ml (2 fl oz/¼ cup) red wine vinegar
125 ml (4 fl oz/½ cup) olive oil,
   plus extra, for pan-frying
4 garlic cloves, chopped

Red rice and beans
60 ml (2 fl oz/¼ cup) olive oil
1 small onion, finely chopped
200 g (7 oz/1 cup) long-grain white rice
375 ml (13 fl oz/1½ cups) chicken stock
60 g (2¼ oz/¼ cup) tomato paste
   (concentrated purée)
400 g (14 oz) tin red kidney beans,
   rinsed and drained

Extras, for adults
chopped coriander (cilantro) leaves,
   to serve

Lay the steak in a glass or ceramic dish. Put the parsley, oregano, vinegar, olive oil and garlic in a food processor with some sea salt and freshly ground black pepper. Process until a coarse paste forms, then pour the mixture over the steak and rub it in well on both sides. Cover and refrigerate overnight.

To prepare the red rice and beans, heat the olive oil in a saucepan over medium heat, then sauté the onion for 5 minutes, or until softened. Add the rice, stock and tomato paste and bring to the boil. Reduce the heat to medium–low, then cover and cook on low heat for 15–20 minutes, or until the rice is tender, adding a little more water if necessary. Remove from the heat and stir in the kidney beans. Cover and leave to stand for 5 minutes, then fluff up the grains with a fork.

Meanwhile, drain the steak well, then pat with paper towels to remove the excess liquid, taking care not to remove any of the herb coating. Heat some more olive oil in a heavy-based frying pan over medium–high heat, then cook the steak for 1–1½ minutes on each side, or until well browned but still a little rare in the middle — take care not to overcook the steak or it will be tough. Transfer to a plate, cover loosely with foil and leave to rest in a warm place for 10 minutes.

Slice the beef into thin strips and serve with the rice.

For the adults, serve sprinkled with coriander.

If the adults prefer a hot chilli version of the Chimichurri marinade, divide the marinade and steak into two portions and add 1 teaspoon chilli flakes to the adult portion.

Chicken satay with peanut sauce and bok choy

You can use cashew nut butter in place of the peanut butter when making the sauce.

2 teaspoons mild curry powder
2 garlic cloves, crushed
1 teaspoon finely grated fresh ginger
125 ml (4 fl oz/½ cup) coconut milk
600 g (1 lb 5 oz) chicken thighs fillets, trimmed and cut into 1 cm (½ inch) pieces
vegetable oil, for brushing
3 baby bok choy (pak choy), leaves separated
steamed jasmine rice, to serve

Peanut sauce

1 teaspoon peanut oil
2 garlic cloves, finely chopped
2 red Asian shallots, finely chopped
125 g (4½ oz/½ cup) crunchy peanut butter (*see tip*)
1 tablespoon fish sauce
1 tablespoon lime juice
1 teaspoon soft brown sugar
125 ml (4 fl oz/½ cup) coconut milk

Put the curry powder, garlic, ginger and coconut milk in a bowl and stir to combine well. Add the chicken, toss to coat all over, then cover and refrigerate for 1–2 hours.

Meanwhile, soak 12 wooden skewers in cold water for 30 minutes to prevent scorching.

Meanwhile, make the peanut sauce. Heat the peanut oil in a small saucepan over medium heat. Add the garlic and shallot and sauté for 1 minute, then stir in the peanut butter, fish sauce, lime juice, sugar and coconut milk and 125 ml (4 fl oz/½ cup) water. Cook, stirring, for 3–5 minutes, or until well combined. Keep warm until required; if the oil starts to separate out, stir in a little more water until combined.

Thread the chicken onto the skewers, making sure the pieces are not too tightly pressed together. Preheat a chargrill pan or large, heavy-based frying pan over high heat, then brush with a little oil. Cook the chicken skewers for 3–4 minutes on each side, or until the chicken is golden and cooked through.

Meanwhile, cook the bok choy in a saucepan of salted water for 2–3 minutes, or until just wilted. Drain well, then chop.

Serve the skewers immediately with the bok choy and the satay sauce for drizzling over, with a bowl of steamed jasmine rice to the side.

Preparation time: 30 minutes
plus 1–2 hours soaking and marinating

Cooking time:
20 minutes

Serves:
2 adults, 2–3 kids

Preparation time: 25 minutes
plus 30 minutes chilling

Cooking time:
30 minutes

Serves:
2 adults, 2 kids

Pork and ricotta rissoles with risoni and braised fennel

2 tablespoons olive oil
1 onion, finely chopped
2 garlic cloves, crushed
600 g (1 lb 5 oz) minced (ground) pork
185 g (6½ oz/¾ cup) firm, fresh ricotta cheese
1 tablespoon dijon mustard
2 egg yolks
55 g (2 oz/½ cup) dry breadcrumbs

Extra rissole seasoning, for adults
¼ teaspoon ground cloves
2 slices of pancetta, finely chopped
1 tablespoon finely sliced sage leaves

Braised fennel, for adults
2 tablespoons extra virgin olive oil
2 fennel bulbs (about 500 g/1 lb 2 oz), cut into thin wedges
250 ml (9 fl oz/1 cup) chicken stock

Risoni
200 g (7 oz/1 cup) risoni (rice-shaped pasta)
80 g (2¾ oz/½ cup) frozen peas
20 g (¾ oz) butter

Heat 2 teaspoons of the olive oil in a small frying pan over medium heat. Add the onion and sauté for 3–4 minutes, or until translucent. Add the garlic and cook for a further minute, then set aside to cool.

Transfer the cooled onion mixture to a bowl and add the pork, ricotta, mustard, egg yolks and breadcrumbs. Season with sea salt and freshly ground black pepper and mix together thoroughly using your hands. Divide the mixture in half and add the extra seasoning for the adults to one half, mixing well. Using damp hands, divide each rissole mixture into eight patties, keeping them separate. Cover and refrigerate for 30 minutes.

For the braised fennel, heat the olive oil in a large frying pan over medium heat. Add the fennel and sauté for 5 minutes, or until light golden. Reduce the heat to medium–low and stir in the stock. Cover and simmer for 3–4 minutes, or until the fennel is tender. Season to taste and keep warm.

Meanwhile, bring a large saucepan of salted water to the boil. Add the risoni and cook for 9 minutes, or until nearly tender. Add the peas and cook for another 2–3 minutes, or until both the risoni and peas are tender. Drain well, then return to the pan with the butter and season to taste. Heat gently to melt the butter, tossing occasionally to coat the risoni. Keep warm.

Heat the remaining oil in a large non-stick frying pan over medium heat. Cook the rissoles in batches for 3–4 minutes on each side, or until golden and cooked through. Serve immediately, on a bed of risoni.

For the adults, serve with the braised fennel.

Chicken san choy bau

4 dried shiitake mushrooms
1 tablespoon peanut oil
½ teaspoon sesame oil
3 teaspoons finely grated fresh ginger
3 garlic cloves, crushed
1 large carrot, cut into fine matchsticks
6 spring onions (scallions), sliced on
   the diagonal
600 g (1 lb 5 oz) minced (ground)
   chicken
60 ml (2 fl oz/¼ cup) oyster sauce
2 teaspoons soy sauce
80 g (2¾ oz/½ cup) tinned water
   chestnuts, drained and chopped
125 g (4½ oz/½ cup) tinned bamboo
   shoots, drained and chopped
220 g (7¾ oz) fresh rice noodles
12 iceberg lettuce leaves, trimmed into
   cup shapes and chilled
Chinese plum sauce (available from
   the Asian section of supermarkets),
   to serve
steamed rice, to serve

Extras, for adults
40 g (1½ oz/¼ cup) toasted cashews,
   chopped

Put the mushrooms in a small bowl and pour in 125 ml (4 fl oz/½ cup) boiling water. Soak for 20 minutes, then drain well. Cut off and discard the tough stems, then finely chop the caps.

Heat the peanut and sesame oil over medium heat in a wok or large non-stick frying pan, swirling to coat the pan. Add the ginger, garlic, carrot and half the spring onion and stir-fry for 1 minute, or until fragrant. Add the chicken and cook for 4–5 minutes, stirring with a wooden spoon to break up any lumps.

Add the oyster sauce and soy sauce and stir-fry for 1 minute, then add the chopped mushrooms, water chestnuts, bamboo shoots and rice noodles. Stir-fry for 2 minutes, or until the noodles have softened and are heated through. Toss the remaining spring onion through.

Spoon the mixture into the lettuce cups and serve immediately with plum sauce and steamed rice.

For the adults, serve sprinkled with the cashews.

Preparation time: 25 minutes
plus 20 minutes soaking

Cooking time:
10 minutes

Serves:
2 adults, 3–4 kids

Preparation time: 20 minutes
plus 15 minutes chilling

Cooking time:
15 minutes

Serves:
2 adults, 2 kids

Noodle soup with fish and prawn dumplings

100 g (3½ oz) vermicelli noodles
1.5 litres (52 fl oz/6 cups) chicken stock
2 tablespoons soy sauce
1 teaspoon fish sauce
1 tablespoon Chinese rice wine (optional)
2 cm (¾ inch) knob of fresh ginger,
    peeled and bruised

Fish and prawn dumplings
200 g (7 oz) white fish fillets, skin and
    bones removed, chopped
100 g (3½ oz) peeled raw king prawns
    (shrimp), cleaned and chopped
50 g (1¾ oz/½ cup) finely sliced sugar
    snap peas
1 tablespoon Chinese rice wine (optional)
1 egg white, lightly beaten
ground white pepper, to taste

Extras, for adults
1 bunch (500 g/1 lb 2 oz) baby bok choy
    (pak choy), chopped
2 long red chillies, finely sliced
2 spring onions (scallions), finely sliced
2 tablespoons soy sauce

Line a baking tray with baking paper.

To make the fish and prawn dumplings, put the fish and prawns in a food processor and blend to a coarse paste. Transfer to a large bowl and add the sugar snap peas, rice wine, if using and egg white. Season with sea salt and ground white pepper and mix together well. Take 1 heaped teaspoon of the mixture and roll it into a ball, placing it on the baking tray. Repeat with the remaining mixture and refrigerate for 15 minutes to firm slightly.

Meanwhile, put the noodles in a heatproof bowl, pour boiling water over and leave to stand for 2 minutes, or until softened. Drain well and set aside.

Pour the stock, soy sauce, fish sauce and rice wine, if using into a large saucepan. Add the ginger and bring to the boil over high heat, then reduce the heat to a simmer. Add the dumplings and simmer for 5–6 minutes, or until cooked through. Remove the ginger and stir in the softened vermicelli noodles.

For the kids, divide a third of the soup, noodles and dumplings between two bowls and serve.

For the adults, add the bok choy to the pan and cook for another 2–3 minutes, or until softened. Meanwhile, mix the chilli, spring onion and soy sauce together in a small bowl. Divide the remaining soup, noodles and dumplings between two bowls and serve the soy sauce mixture on the side as a condiment.

Cook extra bok choy if your children will eat it. You can use any noodles here; some may need pre-cooking before adding to the soup, so check the packet instructions.

Lamb and lentil bolognese with wholemeal spaghetti

185 g (6½ oz/1 cup) brown lentils
80 ml (2½ fl oz/⅓ cup) olive oil
1 large onion, finely chopped
2 carrots, finely chopped
2 celery stalks, finely chopped
200 g (7 oz) Swiss brown mushrooms,
    finely chopped
350 g (12 oz) minced (ground) lamb
    or pork
1½ tablespoons tomato paste
    (concentrated purée)
2 x 400 g (14 oz) tins tomato passata
    (puréed tomatoes)
185 ml (6 fl oz/¾ cup) chicken stock
    or water
500 g (1 lb 2 oz) wholemeal (whole-wheat)
    spaghetti
1 small handful of chopped flat-leaf
    (Italian) parsley

Extras, for adults
35 g (1¼ oz/¼ cup) chopped pitted
    black olives
1½ tablespoons capers, rinsed and
    drained
1 small handful of chopped basil
shaved pecorino cheese, to serve

Place the lentils in a saucepan with enough water to cover, then bring to the boil. Reduce the heat to medium and cook for 35 minutes, or until tender. Drain well.

Meawhile, heat 60 ml (2 fl oz/¼ cup) of the olive oil in a large saucepan. Add the onion, carrot and celery, then cover and cook over medium heat, stirring often, for 12 minutes, or until the vegetables are soft. Add the mushrooms and cook, stirring, for another 4 minutes, or until the mushrooms are soft.

Heat the remaining oil in a large frying pan. Add the lamb and brown well over medium–high heat for 5 minutes, stirring with a wooden spoon to break up any lumps. Add the lamb and any pan juices to the vegetables in the saucepan.

Stir in the tomato paste, passata, lentils and stock. Season to taste with sea salt and freshly ground black pepper and bring the mixture to a simmer. Cook for 25 minutes, stirring often.

Meanwhile, bring a large saucepan of salted water to the boil. Add the spaghetti and cook according to the packet instructions, then drain well and divide among warmed bowls. Stir the parsley into the lentil bolognese.

For the kids, spoon the bolognese sauce over the pasta and serve.

For the adults, stir the olives, capers and basil into the remaining bolognese mixture and spoon over the pasta. Serve scattered with shaved pecorino.

| ❋ **Preparation time:** 25 minutes | ❋ **Cooking time:** 1 hour | ❋ **Serves:** 2 adults, 2–3 kids |

Preparation time:
30 minutes

Cooking time:
2 hours 30 minutes

Serves:
2 adults, 2–3 kids

Braised beef with honey parsnip mash

2 tablespoons olive oil

1 kg (2 lb 4 oz) gravy beef, trimmed and
 cut into 2.5 cm (1 inch) chunks

1 onion, finely chopped

2 garlic cloves, crushed

8 field mushrooms (about 600 g/1 lb 5 oz),
 peeled and cut into 8 slices

375 ml (13 fl oz/1½ cups) tomato passata
 (puréed tomatoes)

1 dried bay leaf

3 tablespoons chopped flat-leaf (Italian)
 parsley

Honey parsnip mash

4 parsnips (about 1 kg/2 lb 4 oz), peeled
 and cut into 4 cm (1½ inch) chunks

1 teaspoon honey, or to taste

½ teaspoon ground cinnamon

20 g (¾ oz) butter

Extras, for adults

2 teaspoons wholegrain mustard

Heat the olive oil in a heavy-based saucepan.
Add the beef in small batches and cook, turning
often, for 5 minutes, or until browned all over,
transferring each batch to a bowl.

Return all the meat to the saucepan. Stir
in the onion and cook for 5 minutes, or until
softened. Add the garlic and mushrooms and
cook for 2 minutes. Stir in the passata and
625 ml (21½ fl oz/2½ cups) water, adding a
little extra water if necessary to just cover the
beef. Add the bay leaf and season with sea salt
and freshly ground black pepper. Bring to the
boil, then reduce the heat to low, cover and
simmer for 2 hours, or until the meat is tender,
stirring occasionally. Adjust the seasoning
if necessary.

Meanwhile, make the honey parnsip mash.
Put the parsnip in a saucepan of salted water and
bring to the boil. Cook for 15 minutes, or until
very tender. Drain the parsnip well, then return
to the saucepan and mash. Stir in the honey,
cinnamon and butter and season to taste.

For the kids, spoon some mash onto warmed
plates, then ladle the braised beef to the side
and sprinkle with parsley.

For the adults, stir the mustard through the
remaining mash before serving.

**If the liquid in the braise needs to be
thickened, remove the meat, bring the
liquid to the boil and allow it to reduce
to the desired consistency. Return the
meat to the sauce to heat through.**

Fish tortillas with a mango and green chilli salsa

If fresh mangoes are unavailable, use a 425 g (15 oz) tin of mangoes, drained and chopped. Instead of tortillas you can make these in jumbo taco shells.

8 soft tortillas
1 tablespoon olive oil
500 g (1 lb 2 oz) firm white fish fillets
  (such as cod, snapper or flathead),
  cut into strips 2 cm (¾ inch) thick
375 ml (13 fl oz) jar of chunky mild salsa
  (available from supermarkets)

For the kids
1 tomato, roughly chopped
150 g (5½ oz/2 cups) shredded iceberg
  lettuce
125 g (4½ oz/½ cup) sour cream

Mango and green chilli salsa, for adults
1 large ripe mango, chopped
1 large green chilli, seeded and finely
  chopped
1 small handful of coriander (cilantro)
  leaves, chopped
1 tablespoon finely chopped red onion
½ teaspoon ground cumin
1 tablespoon olive oil
1 tablespoon lime juice

Put all the mango salsa ingredients in a small bowl and gently mix together. Season to taste with sea salt and freshly ground black pepper, then cover and set aside until required.

Heat the tortillas according to the packet instructions. Keep warm.

Meanwhile, heat the olive oil in a large frying pan over medium heat. Add the fish in batches and cook for 1 minute on each side, or until the fish is almost cooked through. Return all the fish to the pan, add the bottled salsa and gently stir to combine. Heat until warmed through.

For the kids, spread the tortillas with some of the fish mixture and top with the chopped tomato, lettuce and sour cream before rolling up.

For the adults, spread the other tortillas with the remaining fish mixture, top with the mango salsa, then roll up and serve.

✳ Preparation time:	✳ Cooking time:	✳ Serves:
15 minutes	10 minutes	2 adults, 2 kids

Preparation time:
35 minutes

Cooking time:
2 hours 15 minutes

Serves:
2 adults, 2–3 kids

Classic chicken noodle soup

1 small chicken (about 1.5 kg/3 lb 5 oz)
3 large celery stalks
2 large onions
1 dried bay leaf
3 thyme sprigs
30 g (1 oz) butter
3 carrots, finely chopped
3½ tablespoons plain (all-purpose) flour
100 g (3½ oz) dried thin egg noodles
1 small handful of chopped parsley
80 ml (2½ fl oz/⅓ cup) cream
  (optional)
hot buttered toasted baguette slices,
  to serve

Put the chicken in a large saucepan. Chop 1 celery stalk and 1 onion and add it to the saucepan with the bay leaf and thyme sprigs. Add enough cold water to just cover the chicken, then slowly bring to a simmer. Reduce the heat to very low and cook for 1½ hours, skimming off any froth. Do not allow the liquid to simmer quickly or the chicken will be tough. Transfer the chicken to a bowl, allowing any juices to drain back into the pan, then cover and set aside. Skim the excess fat from the stock, then strain, discarding the solids. Measure 1.75 litres (61 fl oz/7 cups) of the stock, adding water to make up the amount if necessary.

Finely chop the remaining celery and onion. Melt the butter in a large saucepan over medium heat and add the celery, onion and carrot. Cover and cook for 10 minutes, or until softened, stirring occasionally. Remove the lid, add the flour and stir constantly for 3 minutes to prevent lumps forming. Increase the heat to medium–high, add 500 ml (17 fl oz/2 cups) of the stock and stir for 2 minutes, or until the mixture thickens. Add 500 ml (17 fl oz/2 cups) more stock and cook, stirring, until it thickens and boils. Continue adding the stock in this way until all the stock is used. Reduce the heat to low and simmer for 20 minutes, stirring often.

Meanwhile, remove the chicken flesh from the bones and skin, then chop finely and add to the soup.

Cook the noodles according to the packet directions. Drain well, then stir into the soup with the parsley and cream, if using. Season to taste and serve immediately, with the toasts.

Try finely chopped fennel instead of the celery, or add cooked frozen peas or corn kernels to the soup with the chicken. Just before serving, stir some finely chopped prosciutto through the adult portions and scatter with some chopped basil or chives.

Thai pork burgers with nahm jim salad

1 tablespoon vegetable oil
400 g (14 oz) tin pineapple rings,
   drained well
2 tablespoons whole-egg mayonnaise
4 hamburger buns, split and toasted
finely sliced cucumber, to serve

Pork patties
1 small red onion, chopped
2 garlic cloves, finely chopped
1 lemongrass stem, white part only,
   finely chopped
1 teaspoon grated fresh ginger
600 g (1 lb 5 oz) minced (ground) pork
1 tablespoon fish sauce
1 carrot, grated
1 egg
40 g (1½ oz/½ cup) fresh breadcrumbs
1 tablespoon Thai red curry paste

Nahm jim salad, for adults
1 green bird's eye chilli, finely chopped
½ small red onion, finely sliced
1 small handful of Thai basil
1 small handful of mint
1 Lebanese (short) cucumber, finely
   chopped
1 teaspoon shaved palm sugar (jaggery)
1 tablespoon lime juice
1 tablespoon fish sauce
2 tablespoons kecap manis (available
   from the Asian section of supermarkets)

To make the pork patties, put the onion, garlic, lemongrass and ginger in a small food processor or blender and process until a paste forms. Scrape the paste into a bowl and add the pork, fish sauce, carrot, egg and breadcrumbs. Season with sea salt and freshly ground black pepper and mix well using your hands.

For the kids, remove one-third of the patty mixture and divide into two even portions, then shape each into a round patty about 10 cm (4 inches) in diameter.

For the adults, mix the Thai curry paste into the remaining mixture and shape into four patties of the same size, keeping them separate.

Heat the oil in a frying pan over medium heat. Add the patties in batches and cook for 6–7 minutes on each side, or until cooked through. Heat a second frying pan over medium heat. Add the pineapple rings, in batches if necessary, and cook for 2 minutes on each side, or until lightly browned.

To make the nahm jim salad, put the chilli, onion, basil, mint and cucumber in a bowl. In a small bowl mix together the palm sugar, lime juice and fish sauce, then pour over the salad and toss to coat.

Spread the mayonnaise on four of the toasted bun rounds and divide among plates.

For the kids, add some cucumber slices, the children's patties and some pineapple to two of the rounds, then put the lids on top and serve.

For the adults, put two patties on each of the remaining rounds. Top with the remaining pineapple, then the nahm jim salad. Drizzle with kecap manis, then put the lids on top and serve.

Preparation time:
25 minutes

Cooking time:
30 minutes

Serves:
2 adults, 2 kids

Teriyaki salmon with pumpkin mash and snow peas

60 ml (2 fl oz/¼ cup) mirin (available from the Asian section of supermarkets)
2 teaspoons sesame oil
80 ml (2½ fl oz/⅓ cup) teriyaki sauce
2 teaspoons sesame seeds, toasted
2 tablespoons vegetable oil
4 x 150 g (5½ oz) salmon fillets, skin and any small bones removed
125 g (4½ oz) snow peas (mangetout), trimmed

Pumpkin mash
750 g (1 lb 10 oz) butternut pumpkin (squash), peeled, seeded and cut into chunks
25 g (1 oz) butter
60 ml (2 fl oz/¼ cup) milk

Extras, for adults
90 g (3¼ oz/1 cup) bean sprouts, tails trimmed
1 spring onion (scallion), sliced on the diagonal

Combine the mirin, sesame oil, teriyaki sauce and sesame seeds in a small bowl. Remove a third of the mixture and reserve for the salad dressing.

To make the pumpkin mash, steam the pumpkin over a saucepan of boiling salted water for 15–20 minutes, or until tender. Drain the pan, add the pumpkin pieces, butter and milk, season to taste with sea salt and freshly ground black pepper and mash well. Cover and keep warm.

Meanwhile, heat the oil in a large frying pan over medium–high heat. Add the salmon, skinned side up, and cook for 2 minutes on each side, or until just cooked through but still a little pink in the middle. Remove from the pan and set aside.

Add the teriyaki mixture to the frying pan and bring to a simmer. Cook over medium heat for 2–3 minutes, or until reduced to a thick glaze consistency. Return the salmon fillets to the pan and gently toss to coat in the glaze.

Meanwhile, put the snow peas in a heatproof bowl and pour over enough boiling water to cover. Leave to stand for 1 minute, or until just softened, then drain well. Reserve three-quarters of the snow peas for the kids.

Thinly slice the remaining snow peas lengthways and toss in a bowl with the bean sprouts and spring onion. Add the reserved teriyaki salad dressing and toss to coat.

For the kids, divide the mash among warmed plates and top each with a piece of salmon. Serve with the plain snow peas.

For the adults, serve the salmon on a bed of mash, with the snow pea salad to the side.

Oven

Lamb with roast tomato sauce and fat rosemary chips • Stuffed baked potatoes • Giant sausage rolls with homemade apple sauce • Baked silverbeet, tuna and pecorino omelette • Honey soy chicken with vegetables and jasmine rice • Baked polenta bolognese • Favourite family pizzas • Lamb chops with carrot and parsnip gratin • Bacon and spinach bake with a tomato, olive and caper relish • Shepherd's pie topped with pea and potato mash • Stuffed pork with radicchio salad • Calzone • Roasted lamb shanks with polenta and sweet and sour capsicum • Crumbed fish with chips and homemade tartare sauce • Sticky spare ribs with fried rice • Individual macaroni cheese and vegetable bakes • Roast chicken and vegetables with salsa verde • Chipolata toad-in-the-hole with tomato and capsicum salsa • Oven-baked paella with saffron chicken drumsticks • Salmon and ricotta cannelloni • Lancashire hotpot • Super-simple ham, tomato and ricotta lasagne • Herbed polenta-coated fish fingers with golden wedges • Beef koftas with raisin, dill and carrot pilaff • Slow-roasted lamb leg with minted yoghurt • Salmon, brown rice and pumpkin patties • Apricot chicken with pine nut parsley crumbs • Meaty nachos topped with avocado cream • Chicken nuggets with parsley mash and homemade barbecue sauce • Big beef and mushroom pie • Tuna, cauliflower and rice bake

Lamb with roast tomato sauce and fat rosemary chips

4 roasting potatoes (900 g/2 lb in total),
  such as russet burbank or sebago
2 rosemary sprigs, leaves picked
1½ tablespoons olive oil
2 x 400 g (14 oz) boneless lamb
  mini (rump) roasts
4 large vine-ripened tomatoes (about
  800 g/1 lb 12 oz in total), halved
6 large unpeeled garlic cloves

Extras, for adults
aïoli, to serve (*see tip*)

Preheat the oven to 200°C (400°F/Gas 6). Peel the potatoes, then cut them into fat chips (fries) about 1.5 cm (⅝ inch) thick.

Line a large baking tray with baking paper (the paper will help the potato chips become crisp during cooking). Scatter the chips and rosemary leaves over the baking paper, drizzle with a tablespoon of the olive oil, toss to coat well and set aside.

Place the lamb roasts on another baking tray and rub all over with the remaining oil. Rub one roast with freshly ground black pepper for the adults. Add the tomatoes to the tray, brush lightly with oil and bake for 15 minutes.

Add the garlic cloves to the roasts and place the tray of chips on the lower shelf of the oven. Bake for 10 minutes, then toss the chips in the oil. Bake for another 20–25 minutes, or until the garlic and tomatoes are tender and the lamb is just cooked. Transfer the lamb to a plate and cover loosely with foil. Remove the garlic and tomatoes from the oven and allow to cool slightly.

Bake the chips for another 10 minutes, or until golden and crisp.

Meanwhile, remove the skin from the tomatoes and squeeze the garlic cloves from their skins. Mash the garlic in a saucepan with the tomatoes and bring to a simmer. Cook over medium heat for 5–6 minutes, or until the mixture has thickened slightly.

Carve the lamb and serve with the chips and roast tomato sauce.

For the adults, top with a spoonful of aïoli.

If aïoli is not available, stir a crushed garlic clove through some whole-egg mayonnaise instead.

Stuffed baked potatoes

✳

You could also top the potatoes with some mashed avocado, sour cream, sweet chilli sauce and grated cheddar cheese.

4 large potatoes (150 g/5½ oz each), such as king edward, sebago or desiree

Bacon, cheese and creamed corn topping
4 slices of bacon, chopped
125 g (4½ oz) tin creamed corn
60 g (2¼ oz/½ cup) grated cheddar cheese
2 tablespoons finely chopped chives

Ricotta, baby spinach and ham topping
1 tablespoon olive oil
1 small red onion, finely chopped
80 g (2¾ oz/½ cup) chopped leg ham
50 g (1¾ oz/1 cup) baby English spinach leaves
160 g (5½ oz/⅔ cup) fresh, firm ricotta cheese
3 spring onions (scallions), finely sliced

Chorizo, tomato and olive topping
2 chorizo sausages, chopped
2 tomatoes (125 g/4½ oz), chopped
40 g (1½ oz/¼ cup) pitted kalamata olives, chopped
2 tablespoons chopped basil
50 g (1¾ oz/⅓ cup) crumbled feta cheese

Preheat the oven to 200°C (400°F/Gas 6). Wash and dry the potatoes, pierce them with a fork, then wrap each one in foil. Bake for 1 hour, or until the potatoes 'give' when gently squeezed. Just before the potatoes are cooked, prepare your desired toppings.

For the bacon, cheese and creamed corn topping, cook the bacon in a non–stick frying pan over medium heat for 3 minutes, or until crisp. Remove from the heat and drain on paper towels. Meanwhile, heat the creamed corn in a small saucepan until warmed through. Transfer to a bowl, stir in the bacon and cheese and sprinkle with the chives.

For the ricotta, baby spinach and ham topping, heat the olive oil in a small frying pan over medium heat, add the onion and cook for 2 minutes, or until softened. Remove from the heat and place in a large bowl. Add the ham, spinach and ricotta and mix well. Sprinkle with the spring onion.

For the chorizo, tomato and olive topping (not shown), place the chorizo in a small cold frying pan over medium heat and cook for 5 minutes, stirring often, until golden. Add the tomatoes and olives and cook for 2 minutes, or until the tomatoes start to soften. Transfer to a bowl and sprinkle with the basil and feta.

When the potatoes are ready, remove them from the oven, remove the foil and cut a cross into the top of each potato. Squeeze them around the middle with your fingers to push open the potatoes. Serve with your choice of topping.

| Preparation time: | Cooking time: | Serves: |
| 20 minutes | 1 hour | 2 adults, 2 kids |

Preparation time:
30 minutes

Cooking time:
1 hour

Serves:
2 adults, 3 kids

Giant sausage rolls with homemade apple sauce

1 teaspoon olive oil

1 onion, finely chopped

2 garlic cloves, finely chopped

1 carrot, finely grated

1 granny smith apple, peeled and grated

300 g (10½ oz) minced (ground) beef

300 g (10½ oz) minced (ground) pork

125 g (4½ oz/1½ cups) fresh breadcrumbs

60 ml (2 fl oz/¼ cup) tomato sauce (ketchup)

1 teaspoon mustard powder

1 teaspoon chopped sage

2 tablespoons chopped flat-leaf (Italian) parsley

2 eggs, lightly beaten

80 g (2¾ oz/½ cup) frozen peas, thawed

2 sheets of frozen puff pastry, thawed

2 teaspoons sesame seeds

Apple sauce

425 g (15 oz) tin pie apples, chopped

125 ml (4 fl oz/½ cup) chicken stock

2 tablespoons vegetable pickle or fruit chutney

Preheat the oven to 220°C (425°F/Gas 7). Line a baking tray with baking paper.

Heat the olive oil in a small frying pan. Add the onion and garlic and sauté over medium–low heat for 3–4 minutes, or until softened. Add the carrot and apple and sauté for another 3–4 minutes, or until soft. Remove from the heat and leave to cool.

Put the onion mixture in a food processor with the beef, pork, breadcrumbs, tomato sauce, mustard, sage and parsley. Process for 1 minute, or until well combined. Add half the egg and process until well mixed. Transfer to a bowl, stir in the peas and season to taste with sea salt and freshly ground black pepper.

Lay the pastry sheets on a lightly floured surface. Divide the meat mixture into two even portions, then shape each into a 'sausage' about 24 cm (9½ inches) long and 7 cm (2¾ inches) wide. Place each sausage in the middle of a pastry sheet, then roll each up to enclose the filling and form two large sausage rolls. Place on the prepared baking tray, seam side down. Using a small sharp knife, make four incisions on top of each roll to allow steam to escape during cooking. Brush the top and sides with the remaining beaten egg and sprinkle with the sesame seeds.

Bake for 10 minutes, then reduce the oven temperature to 200°C (400°F/Gas 6) and bake for another 35–40 minutes, or until the pastry is crisp and golden and the filling is cooked through.

When the rolls are nearly ready, make the apple sauce. Put the apple, stock and pickle in a saucepan over medium heat and cook, stirring, for 5 minutes, or until the liquid has reduced. Serve the sausage rolls thickly sliced, with some apple sauce.

Baked silverbeet, tuna and pecorino omelette

1 kg (2 lb 4 oz/1 bunch) silverbeet
   (Swiss chard), white stalks removed
80 ml (2½ fl oz/⅓ cup) olive oil
½ onion, finely chopped
1 garlic clove, crushed
6 large eggs
80 ml (2½ fl oz/⅓ cup) cream
425 g (15 oz) tin tuna, drained
75 g (2½ oz/¾ cup) grated pecorino
   cheese
40 g (1½ oz/½ cup) fresh
   breadcrumbs
2 tablespoons roughly chopped
   flat-leaf (Italian) parsley

Tomato saffron sauce
2 tablespoons extra virgin olive oil
½ onion, finely chopped
1 garlic clove, crushed
a pinch of saffron threads
3 tomatoes (about 500 g/1 lb 2 oz
   in total), roughly chopped
2 teaspoons honey
½ teaspoon finely grated lemon rind

Preheat the oven to 180°C (350°F/Gas 4).

Wash the silverbeet leaves, drain well, then chop roughly. Place in a large saucepan, cover tightly and cook over medium–high heat for 4–5 minutes, or until completely wilted, shaking the pan now and then. Tip into a colander to drain and cool slightly. Squeeze the cooled silverbeet with your hands to remove as much liquid as possible, then chop finely and set aside.

Heat half the olive oil in a large (26 cm/ 10½ inch), deep heavy-based frying pan. Add the onion and garlic and sauté for 4 minutes, or until softened. Set aside briefly.

In a bowl, whisk together the eggs and cream. Stir in the onion mixture from the pan, as well as the silverbeet, tuna and half the pecorino.

Place the frying pan back over medium heat. Add the remaining oil, swirling to coat the base and side. Pour in the egg mixture, then sprinkle with the breadcrumbs and remaining pecorino. Transfer to the oven and bake for 25 minutes, or until set. Remove from the oven and leave to cool in the pan for 15 minutes.

While the omelette is in the oven, make the tomato saffron sauce. Heat the olive oil in a saucepan over medium heat. Add the onion and garlic and sauté for 3 minutes, then add the saffron, tomato, honey and lemon rind and season with sea salt and freshly ground black pepper. Bring to a simmer, then cook over medium–low heat for 20–30 minutes, or until reduced and thickened.

Carefully run a knife around the edge of the frying pan to loosen the omelette. Invert onto a large plate, then invert onto another plate so the crumbs are on the top. Sprinkle with the parsley, cut into wedges and serve with the saffron tomato sauce.

Preparation time: 20 minutes
plus 15 minutes cooling

Cooking time:
35 minutes

Serves:
2 adults, 2 kids

Preparation time:	Cooking time:	Serves:
30 minutes	1 hour	2 adults, 2 kids

Honey soy chicken with vegetables and jasmine rice

400 g (14 oz/2 cups) jasmine rice
1 tablespoon vegetable oil
1 teaspoon sesame oil
2 small carrots, cut into thin matchsticks
150 g (5½ oz) green beans, trimmed
150 g (5½ oz) snow peas (mangetout),
  trimmed
60 g (2¼ oz/¼ cup) tinned bamboo
  shoots, drained
2 tablespoons oyster sauce
20 g (¾ oz) butter
1 teaspoon sesame seeds

Honey soy chicken
90 g (3¼ oz/¼ cup) honey
60 ml (2 fl oz/¼ cup) soy sauce
2 spring onions (scallions), finely sliced
1½ teaspoons finely grated fresh ginger
2 garlic cloves, crushed
1 teaspoon sesame oil
750 g (1 lb 10 oz) chicken thighs fillets,
  trimmed and cut lengthways into strips
  about 4 cm (1½ inches) thick

Preheat the oven to 180°C (350°F/Gas 4).

To make the honey soy chicken, place a flameproof roasting tin over medium–low heat and add the honey, soy sauce, spring onion, ginger, garlic, sesame oil and 60 ml (2 fl oz/ ¼ cup) water. Cook for about 2 minutes, stirring until the mixture is combined and smooth. Add the chicken pieces and stir to coat well. Transfer to the oven and bake for 45 minutes to 1 hour, or until the sauce has reduced and thickened and the chicken is very tender.

Meanwhile, combine the rice and 500 ml (17 fl oz/2 cups) water in a saucepan. Bring to the boil, then reduce the heat to low, cover and simmer for 15 minutes, or until the water has been absorbed and the rice is tender.

Heat the vegetable oil and remaining sesame oil in a wok or large non-stick frying pan over medium–high heat. Add the carrot and beans and stir-fry for 2 minutes, or until softened slightly. Add the snow peas and bamboo shoots and cook for another minute, or until the vegetables are just tender. Add the oyster sauce and butter and cook for 30 seconds, or until the butter has melted, tossing to combine well.

Divide the rice among warmed plates or shallow bowls. Top with the stir-fried vegetables, then the chicken pieces. Sprinkle with the sesame seeds and serve.

Baked polenta bolognese

2 tablespoons olive oil
1 onion, finely chopped
2 garlic cloves, crushed
500 g (1 lb 2 oz) minced (ground) beef
400 g (14 oz) tin chopped tomatoes
60 g (2¼ oz/¼ cup) tomato paste
  (concentrated purée)
1 teaspoon mixed dried herbs
125 ml (4 fl oz/½ cup) beef stock

Polenta
1 litre (35 fl oz/4 cups) chicken stock
150 g (5½ oz/1 cup) polenta
2 tablespoons pesto
50 g (1¾ oz/½ cup) grated parmesan
  cheese

Extras, for kids
35 g (1¼ oz/¼ cup) grated mozzarella
  cheese

Extras, for adults
1 handful of shredded basil
25 g (1 oz/¼ cup) grated parmesan
  cheese

To make the polenta, bring the stock to the boil in a saucepan. Pour in the polenta in a thin steady stream, stirring constantly. Cook over low heat, stirring constantly, for 10–15 minutes, or until the polenta is very thick and leaves the side of the pan. Stir in the pesto and parmesan and season to taste with sea salt and freshly ground black pepper. Pour the mixture into a greased 19 x 28 cm (7½ x 11¼ inch) tin, smoothing the surface even. Cool to room temperature, then cover and refrigerate for about 30 minutes, or until the polenta is firm.

Meanwhile, preheat the oven to 180°C (350°F/Gas 4). Heat the olive oil in a saucepan over medium heat, then add the onion and sauté for 3 minutes, or until softened. Add the garlic and cook, stirring, for 30 seconds to 1 minute, or until fragrant. Add the beef, breaking up the lumps with a wooden spoon, and cook for 3 minutes, or until it changes colour. Stir in the tomatoes, tomato paste, dried herbs and stock. Bring to the boil, then reduce the heat to medium–low and simmer for 15 minutes, or until the sauce has thickened.

Turn the cooled polenta out onto a board, then cut into long fingers about 3 cm (1¼ inches) thick. Arrange the polenta fingers in a large baking dish, measuring about 23 x 32 cm (9 x 12½ inches). Top with the bolognese sauce.

For the kids, scatter the mozzarella over the top.

For the adults, top with the basil and parmesan.

Transfer to the oven and bake for 20 minutes, or until the cheese is melted and bubbling and the polenta is heated through.

Preparation time: 20 minutes plus about 30 minutes cooling	**Cooking time:** 1 hour	**Serves:** 2 adults, 2–3 kids

Preparation time: 30 minutes
plus 1 hour proving

Baking time:
20 minutes

Serves:
2 adults, 2 kids

Favourite family pizzas

1½ teaspoons active dry yeast
½ teaspoon sugar
150 g (5½ oz/1 cup) wholemeal
 (whole-wheat) flour
185 g (6½ oz/1¼ cups) plain
 (all-purpose) flour
1 teaspoon salt

Ham and pineapple topping
1½ tablespoons tomato paste
 (concentrated purée)
125 g (4½ oz/1 cup) shredded sliced ham
200 g (7 oz/1¼ cups) chopped fresh
 pineapple
200 g (7 oz/1⅓ cups) grated mozzarella
 cheese

Tomato, cheese and chicken topping
1½ tablespoons tomato paste
 (concentrated purée)
1 large tomato, finely sliced
200 g (6 oz/1¼ cups) chopped cooked
 chicken
175 g (6 oz/1¼ cups) grated cheddar
 cheese

Pesto and prosciutto topping
150 g (5½ oz/¾ cup) pesto
200 g (7 oz) mozzarella cheese, finely sliced
90 g (3¼ oz/1 cup) finely sliced
 mushrooms
150 g (5½ oz/8 slices) prosciutto, torn
1 small handful of basil, torn

Put the yeast and sugar in a small bowl with 250 ml (9 fl oz/1 cup) warm water. Leave in a warm place for 10 minutes, or until foamy. Transfer to a large bowl, add the flours and salt and mix until a rough dough forms. Turn out onto a lightly floured surface and knead for 5 minutes, or until smooth and elastic. Place in an oiled bowl, then cover with plastic wrap and leave in a warm place for 1 hour, or until doubled in size.

Preheat the oven to 200°C (400°F/Gas 6). Knock the dough down, then turn out onto a lightly floured surface. Divide into three portions and roll each out to an 18–20 cm (7–8 inch) round. Place on three pizza trays and arrange the toppings over each one. Bake for 20 minutes, or until the dough is crisp and golden and the toppings are bubbling. Cut into wedges and serve.

For the ham and pineapple topping, spread the tomato paste over the pizza bases using the back of a spoon. Sprinkle evenly with the ham and pineapple, then scatter the cheese over the top.

For the tomato, cheese and chicken topping, spread the tomato paste over the pizza bases using the back of a spoon. Arrange the tomato and chicken over the top and sprinkle with the cheese.

For the pesto and prosciutto topping (not shown), spread the pesto over the pizza bases using the back of a spoon. Top with the cheese, mushrooms and prosciutto. After baking, scatter with the basil.

Lamb chops with carrot and parsnip gratin

softened butter, for greasing
2 tablespoons peanut oil
1 garlic clove, crushed
6 lamb shoulder chops (about 1.25 kg/
   2 lb 12 oz in total)
150 g (5½ oz) green beans, trimmed

Carrot and parsnip gratin
2 large parsnips (about 500 g/1 lb 2 oz
   in total), peeled and finely sliced
3 carrots (about 400 g/14 oz in total),
   finely sliced
65 g (2¼ oz/⅔ cup) grated parmesan
   cheese
250 ml (9 fl oz/1 cup) cream

Extras, for adults
60 ml (2 fl oz/¼ cup) red wine
125 ml (4 fl oz/½ cup) beef stock
1 rosemary sprig
20 g (¾ oz) butter

Preheat the oven to 180°C (350°F/Gas 4). Grease a 1.5 litre (52 fl oz/6 cup) baking dish with the softened butter.

To make the carrot and parsnip gratin, bring a pot of lightly salted water to the boil, add the parsnip and carrot and cook for 3 minutes, or until nearly tender. Drain well. Layer half the parsnip and carrot in the baking dish, season with sea salt and freshly ground black pepper, then sprinkle with half the parmesan. Top with the remaining parsnip and carrot, season again, sprinkle with the remaining parmesan and pour the cream over the top. Cover with foil and bake for 40 minutes, then remove the foil and bake for another 20 minutes, or until the parsnip and carrot are very tender.

When the gratin is nearly ready, start cooking the chops. Heat a heavy-based frying pan over high heat. Mix the peanut oil and garlic together in a small bowl, brush the mixture over the chops and season well. Sear the lamb in batches for about 2 minutes on each side, removing each batch to a baking tray. Transfer to the oven and bake for about 3 minutes for medium, or until done to your liking. Cover and keep warm.

Meanwhile, bring a saucepan of salted water to the boil. Add the beans and cook for 2–3 minutes, or until tender. Drain well and keep warm.

For the adults, place the frying pan back over medium heat. Stir in the wine and stock and add the rosemary sprig. Simmer the liquid for 3–5 minutes, or until reduced by half. Remove the rosemary sprig and whisk in the butter.

Divide the chops, gratin and green beans among plates. Drizzle the adult dishes with the rosemary sauce and serve.

Preparation time:
25 minutes

Cooking time:
1 hour 10 minutes

Serves:
2 adults, 2 kids

| ✳ **Preparation time:** 30 minutes | ✳ **Cooking time:** 45 minutes | ✳ **Serves:** 2 adults, 2–3 kids |

Bacon and spinach bake with a tomato, olive and caper relish

40 g (1½ oz/¼ cup) sesame seeds
250 g (9 oz) bacon, cut into 1 cm
  (½ inch) pieces
240 g (6 oz/3 cups) fresh breadcrumbs,
  from a mixed-grain loaf
150 ml (5 fl oz) cream
165 g (5¾ oz/1⅓ cups) grated gruyère
  cheese
3 eggs, lightly beaten
1 small handful of flat-leaf (Italian)
  parsley, chopped
1 large handful of baby English
  spinach leaves, finely chopped

Basic relish
1 tablespoon olive oil
1 onion, finely chopped
1 small carrot, finely chopped
1 garlic clove, finely chopped
2 teaspoons tomato paste
  (concentrated purée)
400 g (14 oz) tin chopped tomatoes
1½ teaspoons caster (superfine) sugar,
  or to taste
2 teaspoons balsamic vinegar, or to taste

Extras, for adults
a pinch of chilli flakes
2 tablespoons chopped pitted green
  olives
1 tablespoon capers, rinsed and
  drained
2–3 tablespoons chopped basil

Preheat the oven to 180°C (350°F/Gas 4).
Grease a 14 x 24 cm (5½ x 9½ inch) baking
dish and scatter with half the sesame seeds.

Heat a non–stick frying pan over medium–
high heat. Add the bacon and cook for
3–4 minutes, or until light golden and cooked
through, stirring often. Remove from the heat.

Put the breadcrumbs, cream, cheese and
eggs in a large bowl and stir well with a fork. Mix
the bacon, parsley and spinach through. Season
to taste with sea salt and freshly ground black
pepper and stir to combine well. Pour the mixture
into the baking dish, smoothing the surface even.
Sprinkle with the remaining sesame seeds and
bake for 40 minutes, or until golden and firm.

Meanwhile, make the basic relish. Heat
the olive oil in a saucepan over medium heat.
Add the onion, carrot and garlic and sauté for
5–6 minutes, or until softened. Add the tomato
paste and cook, stirring, for 1 minute, then
add the tomatoes, sugar and vinegar and stir to
combine. Bring to a simmer, then reduce the
heat to low and cook, stirring occasionally, for
15–20 minutes, or until reduced slightly. Season
to taste and keep warm.

Remove the bacon and spinach bake from
the oven and cut it into slices.

For the kids, serve the bake with some of the
basic relish mixture.

For the adults, stir the chilli flakes, olives, capers
and basil into the remaining relish mixture and
serve with the bake.

Shepherd's pie topped with pea and potato mash

2 tablespoons olive oil
2 carrots, finely chopped
1 large onion, finely chopped
1 large celery stalk, finely chopped
2 garlic cloves, chopped
800 g (1 lb 12 oz) minced (ground) lamb
375 ml (13 fl oz/1½ cups) beef stock
2 tablespoons tomato paste (concentrated purée)
1 tablespoon worcestershire sauce
2 thyme sprigs
1 tablespoon plain (all-purpose) flour
3 tablespoons chopped parsley

Pea and potato mash
750 g (1 lb 10 oz) desiree potatoes, peeled and cut into 5 cm (2 inch) chunks
310 g (11 oz/2 cups) frozen peas
40 g (1½ oz) butter, plus some extra melted butter for brushing
2 tablespoons milk

Preheat the oven to 200°C (400°F/Gas 6).

Heat the olive oil in a large saucepan over medium heat. Sauté the carrot, onion, celery and garlic for 5 minutes, or until softened. Increase the heat to high, then add the lamb and stir constantly for 5–7 minutes until the meat has changed colour, breaking up the lumps with a wooden spoon. Stir in the stock, tomato paste and worcestershire sauce and add the thyme sprigs.

Bring to the boil, then reduce the heat to low and simmer, stirring often, for 20–25 minutes, or until the sauce has reduced. Stir in the flour and cook for another 5 minutes, or until the sauce has thickened. Remove the thyme sprigs, then stir in the parsley and season to taste with sea salt and freshly ground black pepper. Spoon the mixture into a 2 litre (70 fl oz/8 cup) baking dish, or four 500 ml (17 fl oz/2 cup) ovenproof dishes.

While the lamb mixture is simmering, make the pea and potato mash topping. Cook the potatoes in a saucepan of boiling salted water for 15 minutes, or until tender. In a separate saucepan of boiling salted water, cook the peas for 3 minutes, or until tender. Drain the potatoes and peas. Mash the potatoes with the butter and milk and season well. Put the peas in a food processor and blend to a smooth purée, then mix through the potato mash.

Spread the mash over the lamb mixture, using a fork to roughen the surface slightly. Brush the topping with some melted butter, then bake for 20 minutes, or until the topping is golden brown, hot and bubbling. Allow to cool slightly, then serve.

Preparation time:
30 minutes

Cooking time:
1 hour

Serves:
2 adults, 2 kids

Preparation time: 35 minutes
plus 20 minutes resting

Cooking time: 1 hour 30 minutes

Serves:
2 adults, 3 kids

Stuffed pork with radicchio salad

1 kg (2 lb 4 oz/1 bunch) silverbeet
 (Swiss chard), white stalks and
 thick veins removed
2 tablespoons olive oil
1 small onion, finely chopped
2 garlic cloves, finely chopped
2 tablespoons pine nuts
1.5 kg (3 lb 5 oz) pork scotch fillet
apple sauce, to serve
 (see recipe on page 81)
mashed potato, to serve
steamed greens, to serve

Radicchio salad, for adults
2 tablespoons extra virgin olive oil
1 small garlic clove, crushed
½ teaspoon dijon mustard
2 teaspoons red wine vinegar
1 teaspoon honey
1½ tablespoons raisins, chopped
1 head of radicchio, leaves torn

Preheat the oven to 180°C (350°F/Gas 4).

Wash the silverbeet leaves and place in a large saucepan. Cover tightly and cook over high heat for 1–2 minutes, or until wilted, shaking the pan now and then. Transfer to a colander to drain and cool slightly. Squeeze the silverbeet with your hands to remove as much excess liquid as possible, then chop roughly and set aside.

Heat half the olive oil in a saucepan over medium heat. Sauté the onion and garlic for 2–3 minutes, or until softened but not brown. Remove from the heat and add the silverbeet, pine nuts and sea salt and freshly ground black pepper to taste. Mix together well.

Using a large sharp knife, make a horizontal incision about 4–5 cm (2 inches) wide through the pork to create a cavity. Stuff the silverbeet mixture into the cavity, then tie the pork with kitchen string at 2 cm (¾ inch) intervals for a neat shape.

Heat the remaining oil in a heavy–based frying pan over medium heat. Add the pork and cook for 4–5 minutes, or until browned all over, turning often. Place the pork in a baking dish and roast for 1 hour 20 minutes, or until the juices run clear when pierced with a skewer. Remove to a warm place, cover loosely with foil and leave to rest for 20 minutes.

Meanwhile, make the radicchio salad. In a small bowl, whisk together the olive oil, garlic, mustard, vinegar and honey. Stir in the raisins and season with black pepper. Put the radicchio leaves in a salad bowl, pour the dressing over and toss to combine.

Remove the string and carve the pork into thick slices. Divide among plates and serve with mashed potato and steamed greens.

For the adults, serve with the radicchio salad.

Calzone

2 teaspoons active dry yeast
a pinch of sugar
500 g (1 lb 2 oz/3⅓ cups) plain
    (all-purpose) flour, plus extra,
    for dusting
1 teaspoon salt
2 tablespoons olive oil

Filling, for kids
60 ml (2 fl oz/¼ cup) tomato passata
    (puréed tomatoes)
4 thin slices of ham (about 40 g/1½ oz)
100 g (3½ oz/⅔ cup) grated mozzarella
    cheese

Filling, for adults
6 thin slices of prosciutto or salami
1 small handful of rocket (arugula)
2 marinated artichoke hearts, drained
    and cut into quarters
80 g (2¾ oz/⅔ cup) grated fontina
    cheese
100 g (3½ oz/⅔ cup) grated mozzarella
    cheese

Put the yeast and sugar in a small bowl with 150 ml (5 fl oz) warm water. Leave in a warm place for 10 minutes, or until foamy. Transfer to a large bowl, add the flour, salt, olive oil and another 150 ml (5 fl oz) warm water, then mix until a rough dough forms. Turn out onto a lightly floured surface and knead for 5 minutes, or until smooth and elastic. Place in an oiled bowl, then cover with plastic wrap and leave in a warm place for 1 hour, or until doubled in size.

Meanwhile, preheat the oven to 200°C (400°F/Gas 6). Lightly dust a baking tray with a little flour.

Punch the dough down, then divide into four even portions. On a lightly floured surface, roll out each portion into a 25 cm (10 inch) round about 4–5 mm (¼ inch) thick.

For the kids, spread the tomato passata over two of the dough rounds, leaving a 1 cm (½ inch) border around the edge. Arrange the ham slices over the top and sprinkle with the mozzarella.

For the adults, arrange the prosciutto slices over the lower half of the remaining two dough rounds, leaving a 1 cm (½ inch) border around the edge. Top with some rocket, then the artichoke, fontina and mozzarella.

Brush the calzone edges with a little water, then fold the dough back over to enclose the filling. Crimp the edges together to seal well. Place on the baking tray and bake for 12–15 minutes, or until golden brown and crisp.

Preparation time: 40 minutes
plus 1 hour proving

Cooking time:
15 minutes

Serves:
2 adults, 2 kids

| ✳ **Preparation time:** 40 minutes | ✳ **Cooking time:** 1 hour 20 minutes | ✳ **Serves:** 2 adults, 2–3 kids |

Roasted lamb shanks with polenta and sweet and sour capsicum

6 French-trimmed lamb shanks
(about 1.6 kg/3 lb 8 oz in total)
3 garlic cloves, cut into fine slivers
2 tablespoons olive oil
250 ml (9 fl oz/1 cup) chicken stock

Sweet and sour capsicum
60 ml (2 fl oz/¼ cup) olive oil
1 onion, finely sliced
2 garlic cloves, crushed
1 yellow capsicum (pepper), cut into
strips 2 cm (¾ inch) wide
1 red capsicum (pepper), cut into strips
2 cm (¾ inch) wide
1 tablespoon red wine vinegar
3 teaspoons caster (superfine) sugar
400 g (14 oz) tin chopped tomatoes
3 strips orange zest, each about 2 cm
(¾ inch) wide

Extras, for adults
2 anchovy fillets, finely chopped
2 teaspoons capers, rinsed and drained
100 g (3½ oz/⅔ cup) pitted green olives,
roughly chopped

Polenta
500 ml (17 fl oz/2 cups) milk
150 g (5½ oz/1 cup) polenta
40 g (1½ oz) butter
100 g (3½ oz/1 cup) grated parmesan
cheese

Preheat the oven to 200°C (400°F/Gas 6).

Using a small, sharp knife, make deep incisions in the surface of each lamb shank. Push the garlic slivers into the cuts.

Heat the olive oil in a heavy-based frying pan over high heat. Cook the shanks in two batches, for 5–6 minutes, or until browned all over, turning often. Place in a roasting tin and roast for 20 minutes. Pour in the stock, season the shanks with sea salt and freshly ground black pepper and cover with foil. Reduce the oven temperature to 180°C (350°F/Gas 4) and roast for a further 40 minutes, or until the lamb is cooked through. Baste with the pan juices, cover and set aside to rest for 10 minutes.

While the shanks are roasting, prepare the sweet and sour capsicum. Heat the olive oil in a saucepan over medium–low heat. Sauté the onion, garlic and capsicums for 10 minutes. Add the vinegar and sugar and cook for 30 seconds, then stir in the tomatoes and strips of orange zest and simmer gently for 20 minutes, stirring occasionally. Season to taste, remove from the heat and discard the orange zest.

For the kids, set aside half the sweet and sour mix.

For the adults, stir the anchovies, capers and olives into the remaining sweet and sour mixture.

While the shanks are roasting, also prepare the polenta. Put the milk in a saucepan with 500 ml (17 fl oz/2 cups) water and bring to the boil. Reduce the heat to low and add the polenta in a thin, steady stream, stirring constantly to prevent lumps forming. Cook over low heat, stirring often, for 20 minutes, or until the polenta is very thick and comes away from the side of the pan. Stir in the butter and parmesan and season to taste.

Spoon the polenta onto serving plates, place a lamb shank alongside and top with the sweet and sour capsicum mixtures.

Crumbed fish with chips and homemade tartare sauce

35 g (1¼ oz/¼ cup) plain
  (all-purpose) flour
2 eggs
90 g (3¼ oz/1½ cups) panko
  (Japanese breadcrumbs, available
  from supermarkets)
600 g (1 lb 5 oz) thick firm white fish
  fillets (such as ling, blue eye trevalla
  or snapper)
2½ tablespoons vegetable oil
800 g (1 lb 12 oz) roasting potatoes
  (such as russet burbank, sebago or
  spunta), scrubbed
lemon wedges, to serve

Tartare sauce
1 egg yolk
2 teaspoons lemon juice
125 ml (4 fl oz/½ cup) olive oil
1 tablespoon chopped capers
2 gherkins (pickles), finely chopped
1½ tablespoons chopped flat-leaf
  (Italian) parsley

To make the tartare sauce, put the egg yolk and lemon juice in a small food processor and blend until combined. With the motor running, pour in the olive oil in a thin, steady stream and process until the mixture is thick and emulsified. Pour the sauce into a bowl, stir in the capers, gherkin and parsley and season to taste with sea salt. Cover the surface directly with plastic wrap and set aside at cool room temperature until ready to serve.

Preheat the oven to 200°C (400°F/Gas 6). Line two large baking trays with baking paper. Put the flour in a bowl, season with sea salt and freshly ground black pepper and mix well. Break the eggs into another bowl and lightly beat. Tip the panko into a third bowl.

Cut the fish fillets into fingers about 10 cm (4 inches) long and 3 cm (1¼ inches) wide. Toss the fish pieces in the flour, shaking off the excess, then toss them in the beaten egg to coat well, draining off the excess. Finally, coat the fish pieces in the panko, pressing the crumbs on well to make sure the fish is covered. Place on one of the baking trays, cover with plastic wrap and refrigerate for 1 minute to firm the crumbs slightly.

Thinly slice the potatoes and spread on the other baking tray, overlapping slightly if necessary. Drizzle with the oil and season with sea salt and freshly ground black pepper. Transfer to the oven with the fish pieces and bake for 5 minutes. Turn the potato slices over and bake for 5 minutes. Turn again and bake for another 5 minutes, or until the chips are golden and the fish is cooked through.

Serve immediately, with the tartare sauce and lemon wedges.

Preparation time:
45 minutes

Cooking time:
15 minutes

Serves:
2 adults, 2 kids

Preparation time: 25 minutes
plus 30 minutes (or overnight) marinating

Cooking time:
about 1 hour

Serves:
2 adults, 2–3 kids

Sticky spare ribs with fried rice

300 g (10½ oz/1½ cups) long-grain
  white rice
60 ml (2 fl oz/¼ cup) vegetable oil
2 eggs, lightly beaten
2 spring onions (scallions), finely sliced
1 garlic clove, chopped
1 carrot, diced
1 red capsicum (pepper), diced
1 tablespoon soy sauce
1 teaspoon sesame oil

Sticky spare ribs
1 garlic clove, finely chopped
1 lemongrass stem, white part only,
  finely chopped
1 teaspoon grated fresh ginger (optional)
2 teaspoons soy sauce
2 tablespoons kecap manis (sweet soy
  sauce, available from the Asian section
  of supermarkets)
1½ tablespoons honey
1 kg (2 lb 4 oz) pork spare ribs, cut
  into 4 rib sections (ask your butcher
  to do this)

To make the sticky spare ribs, put the garlic,
lemongrass and ginger, if using, in a small food
processor and blend until finely chopped. Transfer
to a large bowl, add the soy sauce, kecap manis
and honey and stir to mix well. Add the ribs, toss
to coat well, then cover and refrigerate for at
least 30 minutes, or overnight.

Wash the rice under cold running water until
the water runs clear. Put the rice and 750 ml
(26 fl oz/3 cups) water in a saucepan over high
heat. Bring to the boil, then reduce the heat to
low, cover and simmer for 15 minutes, or until
the liquid has been absorbed and the rice is
tender. Spread the rice on a tray lined with a
clean tea towel (dish towel). When cool enough
to handle, break up any lumps.

Preheat the oven to 180°C (350°F/Gas 4).
Remove the ribs from the marinade, reserving
the marinade. Place in a roasting tin in a single,
tightly packed layer. Pour in 60 ml (2 fl oz/¼ cup)
water, then bake for 50 minutes, or until the ribs
are tender and dark golden, brushing them often
with the marinade.

Meanwhile, heat 1 tablespoon of the oil in
a wok over high heat. Add the egg and swirl
the wok so it forms a thin layer, then cook for
2–3 minutes, or until set. Turn the omelette out
onto a board. Roll into a tube shape, cut into fine
shreds and set aside.

Heat the remaining oil in the wok. Stir-fry the
spring onion and garlic for 10 seconds. Add the
carrot and capsicum and stir-fry for 2 minutes,
or until tender but still crisp. Add the rice and
toss for 4 minutes to heat through. Mix in the soy
sauce and sesame oil.

Divide the fried rice among serving plates and
top with the egg strips. Cut in between the ribs to
separate them, then arrange over the rice. Drizzle
with the juices from the roasting tin and serve.

Individual macaroni cheese and vegetable bakes

100 g (3½ oz/⅔ cup) macaroni
1 carrot, finely chopped
1 celery stalk, finely sliced
100 g (3½ oz/¾ cup) frozen baby peas

White onion sauce
45 g (1½ oz) butter
1 onion, chopped
2 tablespoons plain (all-purpose) flour
625 ml (21½ fl oz/2½ cups) milk
2 teaspoons dijon mustard
125 g (4½ oz/1 cup) grated cheddar
   cheese

Extras, for adults
100 g (3½ oz) spicy salami, chopped
2 tablespoons chopped basil

Topping
30 g (1 oz) butter
80 g (2¾ oz/1 cup) fresh white
   breadcrumbs
40 g (1½ oz/⅓ cup) grated cheddar
   cheese
35 g (1¼ oz/⅓ cup) grated parmesan
   cheese

Preheat the oven to 190°C (375°F/Gas 5). Lightly oil five small ovenproof dishes, each about 250 ml (9 fl oz/1 cup) capacity, and place on a baking tray.

Bring a large saucepan of salted water to the boil. Add the macaroni and cook for 7 minutes, then add the carrot and celery and cook for another 2 minutes, or until the vegetables are almost tender. Add the peas and cook for 1 minute, then transfer the macaroni and vegetables to a colander and drain well.

To make the white onion sauce, melt the butter in a saucepan, add the onion and sauté over low heat for 4–5 minutes, or until softened but not browned. Add the flour and whisk to a smooth paste. Cook, stirring constantly, for 2–3 minutes, then gradually whisk in the milk until well combined and smooth. Stirring constantly, bring the mixture to a simmer. Continue stirring for 2 minutes, or until the sauce has thickened, then reduce the heat and cook, stirring often, for 5 minutes. Stir in the mustard and cheese and allow to cool slightly.

Mix the macaroni and vegetables through the white sauce and season to taste with sea salt and freshly ground black pepper.

For the kids, spoon the macaroni mixture into three baking dishes.

For the adults, stir the salami and basil through the remaining macaroni mixture, then spoon into the remaining baking dishes.

To make the topping, melt the butter in a frying pan. Remove from the heat, add the breadcrumbs and stir gently to combine. Stir in the cheeses, then sprinkle the mixture over the macaroni mixture. Bake for 20 minutes, or until the topping is golden and crisp. Serve hot.

| ☀ **Preparation time:** 20 minutes | ☀ **Cooking time:** 45 minutes | ☀ **Serves:** 2 adults, 3 kids |

❋ Preparation time:
25 minutes

❋ Cooking time:
1 hour 10 minutes

❋ Serves:
2 adults, 3 kids

Roast chicken and vegetables with salsa verde

300 g (10½ oz) pumpkin (winter squash),
   peeled, seeded and cut into 2.5 cm
   (1 inch) chunks
300 g (10½ oz) orange sweet potato,
   peeled and cut into 3 cm (1¼ inch)
   chunks
10 small roasting potatoes, halved
2 red onions, each cut into 8 wedges
2 tablespoons olive oil
1.6 kg (3 lb 8 oz) free-range chicken
1 lemon, quartered
3 garlic cloves, peeled
1 tablespoon plain (all-purpose) flour
250 ml (9 fl oz/1 cup) chicken stock
310 g (11 oz/2 cups) frozen peas

Salsa verde, for adults

2 garlic cloves, peeled
1 tablespoon small capers, rinsed
   and drained
4 anchovy fillets, drained
2 large handfuls of parsley
1 large handful of mint
1 tablespoon lemon juice
1 tablespoon dijon mustard
60 ml (2 fl oz/¼ cup) extra virgin olive oil

Preheat the oven to 180°C (350°F/Gas 4).

Toss the pumpkin, sweet potato, potatoes and onion in a large bowl with half the olive oil and some sea salt and freshly ground black pepper.

Rinse the chicken well, then pat dry with paper towels. Put the lemon and garlic inside the chicken. Rub the remaining olive oil over the skin and season with black pepper. Place in a large flameproof roasting tin and arrange the vegetables around. Roast for 1 hour, or until the vegetables are golden and the juices run clear from the chicken when tested with a skewer.

Transfer the chicken and vegetables to a large platter and cover with foil to keep warm. Heat the roasting tin on the stovetop over medium heat. Stir in the flour, scraping up any bits stuck to the base of the pan, and cook for 1–2 minutes, stirring constantly. Gradually add the stock, stirring constantly to prevent lumps forming, then bring to the boil. Cook, stirring, for 4–5 minutes, or until the gravy has boiled and thickened.

Meanwhile, bring a small saucepan of water to the boil and add the peas. Cook for 2–3 minutes, or until tender, then drain well.

Put all the salsa verde ingredients in a food processor and blend to a coarse paste. Season with black pepper.

Carve the chicken and serve with the peas and roasted vegetables.

For the adults, serve with the salsa verde.

The salsa verde recipe makes more than you will need to serve with the roast, but it will keep for up to 3 days in an airtight container in the refrigerator. Serve it tossed through pasta with some sliced bocconcini cheese for a quick dinner.

Chipolata toad-in-the-hole with tomato and capsicum salsa

225 g (8 oz/1½ cups) plain
   (all-purpose) flour
500 ml (17 fl oz/2 cups) milk
3 eggs
1 teaspoon roughly chopped rosemary
1 large handful of flat-leaf (Italian) parsley,
   chopped
12 chipolata sausages (about 500 g/
   1 lb 2 oz in total)
4 slices of bacon, cut into thirds
   widthways
100 ml (3½ fl oz) olive oil

Extras, for kids
tomato sauce (ketchup), to serve

Tomato and capsicum salsa, for adults
2 large ripe tomatoes, seeded and finely
   diced
85 g (3 oz/¾ cup) bottled roasted
   capsicums (peppers), finely chopped
1 small red onion, finely chopped
1 tablespoon sweet chilli sauce
1 tablespoon finely chopped flat-leaf
   (Italian) parsley

Put the flour in a bowl with a pinch of salt and the milk. Break the eggs into the bowl and whisk to a smooth batter. Set aside for 30 minutes to rest, then stir in the rosemary and parsley.

Preheat the oven to 220°C (425°F/Gas 7).

Put the chipolatas in a saucepan of cold water. Bring to the boil, then reduce the heat to medium–low and simmer for 3 minutes. Drain well, allow to cool slightly, then wrap a piece of bacon around each chipolata.

Pour the oil into a 5 cm (2 inch) deep baking dish, measuring about 25 x 30 cm (10 x 12 inches). Place the dish in the oven and heat the oil for 15 minutes, or until just smoking. Carefully remove the dish from the oven and pour in the batter. Place the sausages in the dish, then place back in the oven and bake for 20 minutes, or until golden and firm.

Meanwhile, put all the ingredients for the tomato and capsicum salsa in a bowl. Season to taste with sea salt and freshly ground black pepper and mix together well.

Remove the toad-in-the-hole from the oven and serve hot.

For the kids, serve with tomato sauce.

For the adults, serve with the tomato and capsicum salsa.

Preparation time: 20 minutes
plus 30 minutes resting

Cooking time:
45 minutes

Serves:
2 adults, 2–3 kids

Preparation time:
30 minutes

Cooking time:
1 hour

Serves:
2 adults, 3 kids

Oven-baked paella with saffron chicken drumsticks

2 tablespoons olive oil

8 chicken drumsticks (about 1.25 kg/
   2 lb 12 oz in total)

1 onion, chopped

2 garlic cloves, chopped

a large pinch of saffron threads

2 teaspoons ground cumin

2 teaspoons sweet paprika

550 ml (19 fl oz) chicken stock

400 g (14 oz) tin chopped tomatoes

200 g (7 oz/1 cup) long-grain white rice

100 g (3½ oz) bottled roasted capsicums
   (peppers), cut into strips

Extras, for kids

155 g (5½ oz/1 cup) frozen broad
   (fava) beans

Extras, for adults

chopped flat-leaf (Italian) parsley,
   to serve

chopped pitted black Spanish olives,
   to serve

Preheat the oven to 180°C (350°F/Gas 4).

Heat half the olive oil in a large flameproof casserole dish over medium–high heat. Add the drumsticks and cook, turning occasionally, for 5–7 minutes, or until browned all over. Transfer to a plate.

Add the remaining oil, onion and garlic to the casserole dish and sauté for 2–3 minutes, or until softened. Add the saffron, cumin and paprika and stir for 1 minute, or until fragrant. Add the stock, tomatoes, rice, capsicum and drumsticks and mix well. Cover, transfer to the oven and bake for 45–50 minutes, or until the rice and chicken are tender and the liquid is nearly absorbed.

Meanwhile, cook the broad beans in boiling, salted water for 5–6 minutes, or until tender. Drain well, then cool slightly. When the beans are cool enough to handle, peel them.

Divide the paella mixture into two portions.

For the kids, mix the broad beans through the paella and serve.

For the adults, stir the parsley and olives through the paella and serve.

If you are cooking this dish just for adults, you can replace some of the stock with dry white wine.

Salmon and ricotta cannelloni

60 g (2¼ oz) butter
35 g (1¼ oz/¼ cup) plain (all-purpose) flour
875 ml (30 fl oz/3½ cups) milk
125 g (4½ oz/½ cup) ricotta cheese
415 g (14¾ oz) tin salmon, drained, bones and skin removed
1 tablespoon chopped dill, plus extra dill sprigs, to garnish
1 small handful of parsley, roughly chopped
10 dried instant cannelloni tubes
85 g (3 oz/⅔ cup) grated cheddar cheese

Preheat the oven to 180°C (350°F/Gas 4).

Melt the butter in a saucepan over medium–low heat. Add the flour and whisk to a smooth paste. Cook, stirring constantly, for 2–3 minutes, then gradually whisk in the milk until well combined and smooth. Stirring constantly, bring the mixture to a simmer. Continue stirring for 2 minutes, or until the sauce has thickened, then reduce the heat to low and cook, stirring often, for 5 minutes. Allow the sauce to cool slightly.

Pour 250 ml (9 fl oz/1 cup) of the sauce into a bowl and stir in the ricotta, salmon and chopped dill, mixing well. Season to taste with sea salt and freshly ground black pepper.

Stir the parsley into the remaining sauce, season to taste, then spread about 125 ml (4 fl oz/½ cup) of the mixture over the base of a 1.5 litre (52 fl oz/6 cup) rectangular baking dish.

Using two teaspoons or a piping (icing) bag fitted with a plain nozzle, fill each cannelloni tube with the salmon mixture and place in the baking dish. Cover with the remaining sauce and sprinkle with the cheddar.

Bake for 30–35 minutes, or until the cannelloni is soft and the topping is golden and bubbling. Remove from the oven and leave to stand for a few minutes before cutting into serving portions. Serve hot, garnished with dill sprigs.

Preparation time:	Cooking time:	Serves:
20 minutes	50 minutes	2 adults, 2 kids

| | **Preparation time:** 25 minutes | | **Cooking time:** 2 hours 25 minutes | | **Serves:** 2 adults, 2–3 kids |

Lancashire hotpot

1 kg (2 lb 4 oz) boned lamb shoulder, trimmed and cut into 3 cm (1¼ inch) chunks (ask your butcher to do this)

2 tablespoons olive oil

60 g (2¼ oz) butter

2–3 lamb's kidneys, cored, skinned and chopped (optional; *see tip*)

2 onions, finely sliced

1 tablespoon chopped thyme

2 garlic cloves, crushed

1 tablespoon plain (all-purpose) flour

425 ml (15 fl oz) beef stock

1 bay leaf

2 teaspoons worcestershire sauce

6 desiree potatoes (about 900 g/ 2 lb), peeled and cut into 5 mm (¼ inch) slices

Preheat the oven to 170°C (325°F/Gas 3).

Season the lamb well with sea salt and freshly ground black pepper. Heat the olive oil in a deep flameproof baking dish over medium–high heat, then add the lamb in batches and cook for 6 minutes, or until golden all over, turning often. Remove each batch to a plate.

Reduce the heat to medium, then add 20 g (¾ oz) of the butter to the pan. Sear the kidneys, if using, for 1–2 minutes on each side, or until lightly coloured. Remove to a plate.

Add the onion and thyme to the pan and sauté for 5 minutes, or until the onion is translucent. Add the garlic and cook for a further minute, then stir in the flour and cook for 30 seconds. Pour in the stock, stirring constantly to prevent lumps forming. Return the lamb and kidneys to the pan, along with the bay leaf and worcestershire sauce. Adjust the seasoning to taste.

Melt the remaining butter and brush it over both sides of the potato slices. Arrange the potato slices in an overlapping pattern over the meat, then brush the slices again until well coated. Transfer to the oven and bake for 1¾–2 hours, or until the meat is tender and the potato topping is golden and crisp.

To prepare the kidneys, cut them in half lengthways, use a small sharp knife to remove the inner core of fat, then use your finger to peel off the skin. If you are cooking this dish just for adults, replace some of the stock with red wine.

Super-simple ham, tomato and ricotta lasagne

1½ tablespoons extra virgin olive oil

2 garlic cloves, crushed

1 large handful of flat-leaf (Italian) parsley, finely chopped

6 large vine-ripened tomatoes (about 1 kg/2 lb 4 oz in total), cut into 1 cm (½ inch) slices

350 g (12 oz) fresh ricotta cheese

375 ml (13 fl oz/1½ cups) cream

1 egg, lightly beaten

250 g (9 oz/1¾ cups) grated mozzarella cheese

250 g (9 oz) sliced leg ham, off the bone

9 sheets of instant lasagne (about 175 g/ 6 oz in total)

Preheat the oven to 180°C (350°F/Gas 4).

Combine the olive oil, garlic and 1 tablespoon of the parsley in a bowl and season with sea salt and freshly ground black pepper. Add the tomato slices and gently toss to coat. Set aside.

Put the ricotta, cream, egg and remaining parsley in a bowl and beat until smooth using a wooden spoon. Season well.

Lay one-third of the tomato slices in a deep baking dish measuring about 27 x 19 cm (10¾ x 7½ inches). Scatter a quarter of the mozzarella over. Lay one-third of the ham over the mozzarella and spread one-third of the ricotta mixture over the ham. Top with a single layer of lasagne sheets, cutting them to fit if necessary. Repeat the layers with the remaining ingredients, finishing with a sprinkling of mozzarella on top.

Cover with foil, then bake for 25 minutes. Remove the foil and bake for 30–40 minutes longer, or until the cheese is golden and the lasagne is tender. Allow to stand for a few minutes before cutting into serving portions. Serve hot.

Preparation time:
20 minutes

Cooking time:
about 1 hour

Serves:
2 adults, 2–3 kids

| ✳ **Preparation time:** 30 minutes | ✳ **Cooking time:** 30 minutes | ✳ **Serves:** 2 adults, 2 kids |

Herbed polenta-coated fish fingers with golden wedges

4 large sebago potatoes, washed and cut into wedges 1 cm (½ inch) thick
2 tablespoons olive oil
100 g (3½ oz/⅔ cup) plain (all-purpose) flour
150 g (5½ oz/1 cup) polenta
1 small handful of flat-leaf (Italian) parsley, chopped
2 teaspoons finely grated lemon rind
2 eggs
500 g (1 lb 2 oz) firm white fish fillets (such as ling, blue eye trevalla or snapper), cut into fingers 3 cm (1¼ inch) thick
250 g (9 oz/1 cup) whole-egg mayonnaise

Tomato, cucumber and avocado salad
250 g (9 oz) cherry tomatoes, halved
2 Lebanese (short) cucumbers, chopped
1 small red onion, finely sliced
1 small avocado, finely sliced
1 tablespoon lemon juice
1 tablespoon olive oil

Extras, for adults
1 tablespoon capers, finely chopped
1½ tablespoons finely chopped gherkins (pickles)
1 tablespoon finely chopped flat-leaf (Italian) parsley
½ teaspoon finely grated lemon rind
lemon wedges, to serve

Preheat the oven to 200°C (400°F/Gas 6). Line one baking tray with baking paper and lightly oil another baking tray.

Spread the potato wedges on the lined baking tray and drizzle with the olive oil. Season with sea salt and bake for 15 minutes.

Meanwhile, put the flour in a shallow bowl, and in another shallow bowl mix the polenta, parsley and lemon rind. Break the eggs into a third bowl and lightly beat. Dust the fish pieces in the flour, shaking off the excess, then coat them in the egg, allowing the excess to drain off. Finally, coat the fish in the polenta mixture, pressing gently to coat all over.

Spread the fish pieces on the oiled baking tray and bake with the wedges for another 15 minutes, or until the fish is cooked through, and the crumbs and wedges are golden and crisp.

Meanwhile, gently toss all the ingredients for the tomato, cucumber and avocado salad in a serving bowl and season to taste.

Divide the mayonnaise among two small serving bowls.

For the kids, serve the fish fingers with the potato wedges, salad and plain mayonnaise.

For the adults, mix the capers, gherkins, parsley and lemon rind into the remaining bowl of mayonnaise and season to taste with freshly ground black pepper. Serve with the fish fingers, salad and lemon wedges.

Beef koftas with raisin, dill and carrot pilaff

Raisin, dill and carrot pilaff
400 g (14 oz/2 cups) long-grain white rice
60 g (2¼ oz) unsalted butter
1 tablespoon olive oil
2 carrots, finely diced
1 teaspoon dill seeds
30 g (1 oz/¼ cup) raisins
250 ml (9 fl oz/1 cup) chicken stock

Beef koftas
750 g (1 lb 10 oz) minced (ground) beef
1 slice of stale bread, torn into chunks
½ teaspoon ground allspice
1 teaspoon ground cumin
1 garlic clove, chopped
1 small onion, diced
1 handful of flat-leaf (Italian) parsley
½ teaspoon salt
250 ml (9 fl oz/1 cup) tomato passata
  (puréed tomatoes)

Preheat the oven to 180°C (350°F/Gas 4).

To make the raisin, dill and carrot pilaff, wash the rice under cold running water until the water runs clear, then drain well in a colander and set aside.

Heat the butter and olive oil in a flameproof casserole dish over medium heat. Add the diced carrot, stir to coat in the butter, then sauté for 5 minutes. Add the dill seeds and rice, stirring for a minute or until the rice is transparent. Scatter the raisins over the top, pour in the stock and 625 ml (21½ fl oz/2½ cups) water, then cover and bring to the boil. Transfer to the oven and cook for 20 minutes. Remove from the oven, leave the lid on and leave to stand in a warm place.

Meanwhile, make the beef koftas. Put the beef, bread, spices, garlic, onion, parsley and salt in a food processor, season with freshly ground black pepper and blend until well combined. With moistened hands, roll heaped tablespoons of the kofta mixture into about 16 balls. Place in a baking dish that is large enough to comfortably fit them all side by side. Mix the tomato passata with 250 ml (9 fl oz/1 cup) boiling water and pour over the meatballs. Cover with foil and bake for 15 minutes, or until the meatballs are cooked through.

Stir the raisins through the pilaff to mix well, then spoon a mound of rice onto serving plates. Top with the meatballs, spoon the juices from the baking dish over the top and serve.

<table>
| ☀ | **Preparation time:** 15 minutes
plus 10 minutes resting | ☀ | **Cooking time:**
30 minutes | ☀ | **Serves:**
2 adults, 2–3 kids |
</table>

Preparation time: 40 minutes
plus 30 minutes soaking

Cooking time:
2 hours 10 minutes

Serves: 2 adults,
3 kids (with some leftover)

Slow-roasted lamb leg with minted yoghurt

1.5 kg (3 lb 5 oz) leg of lamb, bone in, rinsed and dried
125 ml (4 fl oz/½ cup) olive oil
3 pontiac potatoes (about 325 g/ 11½ oz), peeled and cut into 3 cm (1¼ inch) chunks
1 red onion, cut into 3 cm (1¼ inch) chunks
1 red capsicum (pepper), cut into 3 cm (1¼ inch) chunks
1 zucchini (courgette), cut into 3 cm (1¼ inch) chunks
1 eggplant (aubergine), cut into 2 cm (¾ inch) rounds
1 small handful of rocket (arugula)

Minted yoghurt, for adults
125 g (4½ oz/½ cup) Greek-style yoghurt
1 small handful of chopped mint
1 tablespoon lemon juice

Pan gravy
350 ml (12 fl oz) beef stock
1½ tablespoons cornflour (cornstarch)

Put the minted yoghurt ingredients in a bowl, season to taste with sea salt and mix well. Cover and refrigerate until required.

Preheat the oven to 200°C (400°F/Gas 6). Put the lamb in a flameproof roasting tin, rub with 1 tablespoon of the olive oil, sprinkle with sea salt and roast for 30 minutes. Reduce the oven temperature to 160°C (315°F/Gas 2–3).

Put the potato, onion, capsicum and zucchini in a small roasting tin and drizzle with 1 tablespoon of the oil. Roast with the lamb for a further 1½ hours, or until the lamb is medium–rare and the vegetables are golden and tender. Transfer the lamb to a plate, cover loosely with foil and rest in a warm place.

Meanwhile, sprinkle the eggplant with salt and leave in a colander for 30 minutes to drain. Rinse the eggplant, drain well, then pat dry with paper towels. Heat the remaining oil in a large frying pan and cook the eggplant over medium heat, in batches if necessary, for 10 minutes, or until dark golden, turning occasionally. Drain on paper towels and leave to cool, then roughly chop.

To make the pan gravy, pour off the excess fat from the roasting tin, taking care to retain the meat juices. Place the tin over medium heat and add the stock. Bring to the boil, stirring to remove any stuck-on bits, then reduce the heat and simmer gently for 5 minutes. Mix the cornflour to a smooth paste with 1 tablespoon water, then add it to the pan, stirring constantly until the gravy boils and thickens.

For the kids, serve the lamb with the pan gravy and roasted vegetables.

For the adults, toss the eggplant and rocket with the roasted vegetables, then serve with the lamb, pan gravy and minted yoghurt.

If you are cooking this dish just for adults, you can replace some of the stock with dry red wine.

Salmon, brown rice and pumpkin patties

1 tablespoon miso paste (available from
   the Asian section of supermarkets)
1 tablespoon finely grated fresh ginger
125 ml (4 fl oz/½ cup) vegetable oil
½ small jap pumpkin (winter squash)
   (about 600 g/1 lb 5 oz), peeled and
   cut into 2 cm (¾ inch) chunks
200 g (7 oz/1 cup) long-grain brown rice
20 g (¾ oz) butter
415 g (14¾ oz) tin pink salmon, drained
   and flaked with a fork
2 tablespoons chopped coriander (cilantro)
2 teaspoons soy sauce or tamari
75 g (2½ oz/½ cup) plain (all-purpose)
   flour
155 g (5½ oz/1 cup) sesame seeds
1 egg
2 tablespoons milk

Ginger glaze
2 teaspoons sesame oil
2 teaspoons soy sauce or tamari
2 red Asian shallots, sliced
2 garlic cloves, chopped
2 teaspoons finely grated fresh ginger
125 ml (4 fl oz/½ cup) mirin (available
   from Asian food stores)
2 tablespoons caster (superfine) sugar

Preheat the oven to 180°C (350°F/Gas 4).
Line a baking tray with baking paper.

In a bowl combine the miso paste, ginger
and 1 tablespoon of the vegetable oil. Add
the pumpkin and toss to coat, then spread
on the baking tray in a single layer. Bake for
30 minutes, or until tender, then remove from
the oven and allow to cool slightly.

Meanwhile bring 1.5 litres (52 fl oz/6 cups)
water to the boil in a saucepan. Add the rice
and butter and boil, uncovered, for 45 minutes,
or until tender, adding a little more water if
necessary. Drain well, then rinse briefly under
cold running water. Leave to cool, then transfer
to a bowl with the pumpkin, salmon, coriander
and soy sauce and mix together well. Using
damp hands, form into eight even patties, about
6 cm (2½ inches) in diameter. Refrigerate for
30 minutes, or until firm.

Put the flour in a bowl, and the sesame seeds
in another bowl. In a third bowl, whisk together
the egg and milk. Working one at a time, dust the
patties with the flour, shaking off the excess. Dip
them into the egg mixture, allowing the excess to
drain off, then dip them into the sesame seeds,
pressing gently to coat. Transfer to a tray, then
cover and refrigerate for another 30 minutes, or
until the coating is firm.

Heat the remaining oil in a frying pan over
medium heat. Cook the patties in two batches
for about 2 minutes on each side, or until lightly
golden. Transfer to a baking tray and bake for
10 minutes, or until heated through.

Meanwhile, put the ginger glaze ingredients
in a saucepan. Bring to the boil, then reduce the
heat to medium–low and simmer for 2 minutes,
or until the mixture has reduced and thickened.
Serve the hot patties with a mixed salad and the
ginger glaze spooned over.

Preparation time: 30 minutes
plus 1 hour chilling

Cooking time:
1 hour 10 minutes

Serves:
2 adults, 3 kids

Preparation time:
30 minutes

Cooking time:
1 hour

Serves:
2 adults, 2 kids

Apricot chicken with pine nut parsley crumbs

75 g (2½ oz/½ cup) plain (all-purpose)
  flour
1.6 kg (3 lb 8 oz) chicken, cut into
  10 pieces (or use the equivalent weight
  of drumsticks and thighs on the bone)
80 ml (2½ fl oz/⅓ cup) olive oil
1 large onion, cut into thin wedges
1 garlic clove, crushed
1 tablespoon finely chopped rosemary
400 ml (14 fl oz) tin apricot nectar
90 g (3¼ oz/½ cup) dried apricots, halved
400 g (14 oz) baby new potatoes, halved
500 g (1 lb 2 oz) broccolini, trimmed

Pine nut parsley crumbs, for adults
40 g (1½ oz) butter
40 g (1½ oz/½ cup) fresh wholemeal
  (whole-wheat) breadcrumbs
1 garlic clove, crushed
1 tablespoon roughly chopped pine nuts
1 small handful of chopped flat-leaf
  (Italian) parsley

Preheat the oven to 180°C (350°F/Gas 4).

Put the flour in a shallow dish and season with sea salt and freshly ground black pepper. Toss the chicken pieces in the flour, shaking off the excess. Heat 2 tablespoons of the olive oil in a flameproof casserole dish over medium–high heat. Add the chicken in batches and cook for 2–3 minutes on each side, or until golden. Transfer each batch to a plate and set aside.

Heat another tablespoon of the oil in the casserole dish. Sauté the onion, garlic and rosemary for 3–4 minutes, or until the onion has softened. Add the apricot nectar and apricots. Bring to the boil, then reduce the heat to medium. Return the chicken pieces to the dish. Cover the dish, transfer to the oven and bake for 15 minutes.

Toss the potatoes in the remaining olive oil with some sea salt and cracked black pepper. Place on a baking tray and roast with the chicken for a further 25–30 minutes, or until the potatoes are golden and the chicken is tender.

Near serving time, make the pine nut parsley crumbs. Melt the butter in a frying pan over medium heat, add the breadcrumbs and stir until coated. Add the garlic and pine nuts and cook for 2–3 minutes, or until golden brown. Remove from the heat and stir in the parsley.

Meanwhile, cook the broccolini in a large saucepan of salted boiling water for 3 minutes, or until tender. Drain well.

For the kids, serve the chicken with the potatoes and broccolini.

For the adults, sprinkle the pine nut parsley crumbs over the broccolini and serve with the chicken and potatoes.

Meaty nachos topped with avocado cream

800 g (1 lb 12 oz) tin chopped tomatoes
1 small handful of coriander (cilantro)
    leaves
1 large mild green banana chilli or
    small green capsicum (pepper),
    seeds removed, flesh chopped
1 tablespoon peanut oil
4 spring onions (scallions), finely sliced
1 garlic clove, crushed
2 teaspoons mild paprika
1½ teaspoons ground cumin
1 teaspoon dried oregano
500 g (1 lb 2 oz) minced (ground) beef
1 tablespoon tomato paste (concentrated
    purée)
1 large packet (200 g/7 oz) plain corn
    chips
310 g (11 oz/2½ cups) grated cheddar
    cheese
125 g (4½ oz/½ cup) sour cream
2 roma (plum) tomatoes, chopped

Avocado cream

1 large ripe avocado
1 tablespoon lemon juice
125 g (4½ oz/½ cup) sour cream

Extras, for adults

Tabasco sauce, to taste
sliced jalapeño chillies, to serve
2 spring onions (scallions), finely sliced
coriander (cilantro) leaves, to serve

Preheat the oven to 180°C (350°F/Gas 4).

Put the tomatoes, coriander and green chilli or capsicum in a food processor and blend until smooth.

Heat the peanut oil in a large frying pan over medium–high heat. Add the spring onion, garlic, spices and oregano and cook, stirring, for 1 minute. Add the beef and cook for 3–4 minutes, or until golden, breaking up the lumps with a wooden spoon. Add the tomato paste and puréed tomato mixture, then reduce the heat and simmer for 5 minutes, or until thickened slightly. Season to taste with sea salt and freshly ground black pepper.

Spread half the corn chips in a large deep baking dish (about 20 x 32 cm/8 x 12½ inches). Spoon half the beef mixture over and sprinkle with half the cheese. Repeat with the remaining corn chips and beef mixture, then scatter the remaining cheese over the top. Bake on the top shelf of the oven for 20–25 minutes, or until the cheese is golden and bubbling. Remove from the oven.

To make the avocado cream, put the avocado and lemon juice in a bowl and mash well with a fork. Add the sour cream, mash until smooth, then season to taste.

Divide the nachos among serving bowls. Add a dollop of avocado cream, then a spoonful of sour cream.

For the kids, scatter the chopped tomatoes over the top and serve.

For the adults, sprinkle with Tabasco and serve scattered with some jalapeño chilli, spring onion and coriander.

| ✳ **Preparation time:** 20 minutes | ✳ **Cooking time:** 35 minutes | ✳ **Serves:** 2 adults, 2–3 adults |

Preparation time:	**Cooking time:**	**Serves:**
25 minutes	25 minutes	2 adults, 2 kids

Chicken nuggets with parsley mash and homemade barbecue sauce

600 g (1 lb 5 oz) chicken thighs fillets, trimmed

35 g (1¼ oz/¼ cup) plain (all-purpose) flour

2 eggs

160 g (5¾ oz/2 cups) fresh breadcrumbs

2 tablespoons finely grated parmesan cheese

1 tablespoon finely chopped flat-leaf (Italian) parsley

2½ tablespoons olive oil

Barbecue sauce

250 ml (9 fl oz/1 cup) tomato passata (puréed tomatoes)

2½ tablespoons soft brown sugar

½ teaspoon worcestershire sauce

1 tablespoon balsamic vinegar

1 tablespoon American or other mild mustard

Tabasco sauce, to taste (optional)

Parsley mash

800 g (1 lb 12 oz) desiree potatoes

75 g (2½ oz) butter, chopped

80 ml (2½ fl oz/⅓ cup) milk

1 small handful of chopped flat-leaf (Italian) parsley

Rocket, tomato and olive salad, for adults

1 handful of rocket (arugula)

1 roma (plum) tomato, cut into wedges

½ avocado, cut into 2 cm (¾ inch) chunks

40 g (1½ oz/¼ cup) kalamata olives

1 tablespoon lemon juice

2 tablespoons extra virgin olive oil

Preheat the oven to 200°C (400°F/Gas 6). Line a roasting tin with foil and lightly oil the foil.

Put all the barbecue sauce ingredients in a saucepan and stir together well. Bring to a simmer, then cook over medium–low heat for 10 minutes, or until reduced and thickened slightly, stirring often. Remove from the heat, season to taste with sea salt and leave to cool. Cover and set aside.

Meanwhile, prepare the chicken nuggets. Cut the chicken thighs into strips about 2 cm (¾ inch) wide. Put the flour in a shallow bowl and season with sea salt and freshly ground black pepper. Break the eggs into another bowl and whisk in 1½ tablespoons water. In a third bowl mix together the breadcrumbs, parmesan and parsley. Toss the chicken strips in the flour, shaking off the excess. Toss them in the egg mixture, draining off the excess, then toss in the breadcrumb mix to coat well.

Place the nuggets in the roasting tin and drizzle with the olive oil. Bake on the middle shelf of the oven for 20–25 minutes, or until the nuggets are golden and cooked through, turning them over halfway during cooking.

Meanwhile, make the parsley mash. Peel and chop the potatoes, then cook in a saucepan of boiling salted water for 15 minutes, or until tender. Drain well, then return to the saucepan and mash until smooth using a potato masher. Add the butter and milk, season to taste and stir until the butter has melted through. Cover and keep warm, stirring in the parsley just before serving.

For the kids, serve the nuggets and mash with the barbecue sauce.

For the adults, put the salad ingredients in a bowl, toss gently and serve with the nuggets, mash and barbecue sauce.

Big beef and mushroom pie

35 g (1¼ oz/¼ cup) plain (all-purpose) flour
60 ml (2 fl oz/¼ cup) olive oil
1 kg (2 lb 4 oz) chuck steak, trimmed and cut into 1.5 cm (⅝ inch) chunks
1 large onion, finely sliced
250 g (9 oz/2¾ cups) sliced button mushrooms
2 tablespoons thyme
2 garlic cloves, crushed
275 ml (5 fl oz) beef stock
2 teaspoons worcestershire sauce
2 teaspoons wholegrain mustard
2 sheets of frozen puff pastry, thawed
1 egg, lightly beaten

Put the flour in a shallow bowl and season well with sea salt and freshly ground black pepper. Add the steak, in batches if necessary, and toss to coat, shaking off the excess.

Heat 2 tablespoons of the olive oil in a flameproof casserole dish over medium–high heat. Add the steak in batches and sear for 1–2 minutes on each side, or until golden brown, adding more oil if necessary. Remove each batch to a plate.

Reduce the heat to medium–low. Add any remaining oil to the dish and sauté the onion for 5–6 minutes, or until translucent. Add the mushrooms, thyme and garlic and sauté for a further 2–3 minutes, or until the mushrooms have softened. Return the beef to the dish, stir in the stock, worcestershire sauce and mustard and bring to the boil. Reduce heat, cover and simmer on medium–low for 1 hour, or until the meat is very tender.

Transfer the beef mixture to a 1.25 litre (44 fl oz/5 cup) round pie dish (about 27 cm/10¾ inches across the top, 16 cm/6¼ inches across the base and 6 cm/2½ inches high). Allow to cool for 10 minutes, then cover and refrigerate for 1 hour, or until cold.

Preheat the oven to 200°C (400°F/Gas 6). From one sheet of pastry, cut four long strips, each 5 mm (¼ inch) wide. Place these around the edge of the pie dish, overlapping where necessary. Brush with beaten egg, then carefully cover the filling with the remaining pastry and press the edges to seal. (Cut the remaining pastry to fill in any gaps.) Trim the overhanging pastry, brush the top generously with egg, then cut two small slits into the top of the pie to allow steam to escape.

Bake for 40 minutes, or until the pastry is golden. Serve warm.

✳ **Preparation time:** 30 minutes
plus 1 hour chilling

✳ **Cooking time:**
2 hours 15 minutes

✳ **Serves:**
2 adults, 2–3 kids

Tuna, cauliflower and rice bake

220 g (7¾ oz/1 cup) short-grain
  brown rice
100 g (3½ oz) baby English spinach
  leaves
60 g (2¼ oz) butter
1 onion, finely chopped
1 garlic clove, crushed
½ cauliflower (about 400 g/14 oz in total),
  cut into small florets
2 tablespoons plain (all-purpose) flour
250 ml (9 fl oz/1 cup) milk
185 g (6½ oz) tin tuna, drained
1 teaspoon freshly grated nutmeg
60 g (2¼ oz/½ cup) grated cheddar
  cheese
40 g (1½ oz/½ cup) fresh breadcrumbs
3 tablespoons chopped flat-leaf (Italian)
  parsley

Preheat the oven to 180°C (350°F/Gas 4).

Put the rice in a saucepan, then place under cold running water until the water runs clear. Drain the rice well and return to the pan with 625 ml (21½ fl oz/2½ cups) water. Cover the saucepan, bring to a simmer, then reduce the heat to low and cook the rice for 30 minutes, or until tender. Drain again, stir in the spinach, then transfer the mixture to a 1 litre (35 fl oz/4 cup) baking dish, or four 375 ml (13 fl oz/1½ cup) ramekins.

Melt 20 g (¾ oz) of the butter in a large saucepan over medium heat. Add the onion and sauté for 3–4 minutes, or until starting to brown, then add the garlic and continue to cook for 1–2 minutes. Add the cauliflower, stir to combine, then cover and cook, stirring occasionally, for 8–10 minutes, or until softened.

Meanwhile, melt the remaining butter in a saucepan over medium–low heat. Add the flour and whisk to a smooth paste. Cook, stirring constantly, for 2–3 minutes, then gradually whisk in the milk until well combined and smooth. Stirring constantly, bring the mixture to a simmer. Continue stirring for 2 minutes, or until the sauce has thickened, then reduce the heat to low and cook, stirring often, for 5 minutes.

Pour the sauce into the cauliflower mixture, then add the tuna and mix until well combined. Pour onto the rice mixture and sprinkle with the combined cheese and breadcrumbs.

Bake for 25–30 minutes, or until the topping is golden. Serve hot, sprinkled with the parsley.

Desserts

Plum and polenta roly poly • Orange-berry trifles • Apple and oat crumble • Sweet baked ricotta cake with cherries • Jaffa steamed pudding with chocolate sauce • Grape jelly with whipped cream and fennel • Chocolate brownie ice cream sandwiches • Apricot sponge pudding • Chocolate-dipped ice cream balls • Golden syrup coconut dumplings with lime custard • Caramel banana splits • Rocky road ice cream terrine • Date, raisin and pecan loaf • Milk and honey jellies with sherry jelly • Banana fritters • Apple and peach turnovers • White chocolate mousse with strawberries • Brown sugar rice pudding with prune compote • Lemon crepes • Pear, caramel and pecan sundaes • Yoghurt, coconut and apricot ice cream sticks • Rich chocolate puddings • Tropical Eton mess • Watermelon, cranberry and lime granita

Preparation time:
25 minutes

Cooking time:
40 minutes

Serves:
2 adults, 3 kids (with leftovers)

Plum and polenta roly poly

60 g (2¼ oz/½ cup) raisins
75 g (2½ oz/½ cup) currants
315 g (11 oz/1 cup) plum jam
½ teaspoon ground cinnamon
1 teaspoon finely grated orange rind
225 g (8 oz/1½ cups) plain
 (all-purpose) flour
3 teaspoons baking powder
75 g (2½ oz/½ cup) polenta
75 g (2½ oz) unsalted butter, chopped
250 g (9 oz/1 cup) sour cream
sifted icing (confectioners') sugar,
 for dusting
custard, to serve
whipped cream, to serve

Extras, for adults
Cointreau or other orange-flavoured
 liqueur, to taste (optional)

Preheat the oven to 180°C (350°F/Gas 4).

Put the raisins, currants, jam, cinnamon and orange rind in a bowl and mix together well. Set aside.

Sift the flour and baking powder into a bowl, then stir in the polenta. Using your fingertips, rub the butter in until the mixture resembles coarse breadcrumbs. Using a flat-bladed knife, stir in the sour cream until a rough dough forms, adding 1–2 tablespoons cold water if necessary.

Roll the dough out on a floured surface into a rectangle measuring about 35 x 26 cm (14 x 10½ inches). Spread the jam mixture over the dough, leaving a 1.5 cm (⅝ inch) border around the edge. Brush the border with a little cold water.

Starting with a longer edge, roll the dough up to form a 'log' about 35 cm (14 inches) long. Cut a sheet of baking paper a little longer than the roly poly, then carefully transfer the roly poly to the baking paper. Roll the log in the paper to enclose, leaving a little space for the roly poly to expand during baking. Twist both ends to close.

Place the log on a baking tray and bake for 35–40 minutes, or until light golden and firm. Leave to cool for 5–10 minutes, then carefully remove the paper.

Cut the roly poly into diagonal slices using a serrated knife. Dust generously with icing sugar and serve with custard and whipped cream.

For the adults, stir a little liqueur into the custard, if desired.

Orange-berry trifles

375 ml (13 fl oz/1½ cups) custard
250 ml (9 fl oz/1 cup) cream, whipped
1 teaspoon finely grated orange rind
60 ml (2 fl oz/¼ cup) orange juice
1 tablespoon caster (superfine) sugar
8 savoiardi (lady finger/sponge finger) biscuits
155 g (5½ oz/1¼ cups) raspberries
155 g (5½ oz/1 cup) blueberries or strawberries, hulled and sliced, plus extra, to decorate
grated dark chocolate, for sprinkling

Extras, for adults
2 tablespoons Grand Marnier (orange-flavoured liqueur) or sherry
2 tablespoons flaked almonds, lightly toasted

Put the custard, whipped cream and orange rind in a large bowl with 1 tablespoon of the orange juice and 2 teaspoons of the sugar. Stir gently to just combine, then cover and refrigerate until required.

Divide the biscuits among two large plates.

For the kids, sprinkle half of the biscuits with the remaining orange juice.

For the adults, sprinkle the other biscuits with the liqueur or sherry. Leave for 10–15 minutes, to allow the liquid to be absorbed.

Put all the berries in a bowl with the remaining sugar and lightly mash with a fork.

Break each biscuit into three pieces. Take four deep, 375 ml (13 fl oz/1½ cups) glasses or glass bowls and place three biscuit pieces in each. Spoon over half the berry mixture, then half the custard mixture. Repeat the layering with three more biscuit pieces and the remaining berries and custard.

For the kids, sprinkle the trifles with a little grated chocolate.

For the adults, sprinkle with the flaked almonds.

Cover and refrigerate for at least 2 hours to allow the flavours to develop. Decorate with more berries just before serving.

Preparation time: 20 minutes
plus 2 hours chilling

Cooking time:
nil

Serves:
2 adults, 2 kids

Preparation time: 15 minutes	**Cooking time:** 40 minutes	**Serves:** 2 adults, 3 kids

Apple and oat crumble

melted butter, for greasing
6 granny smith apples (about 1.2 kg/
  2 lb 12 oz in total)
2 tablespoons lemon juice
2 tablespoons caster (superfine) sugar
whipped cream or vanilla ice cream,
  to serve

Crumble topping
3 slices of day-old white bread, crusts
  removed
50 g (1¾ oz/½ cup) rolled (porridge) oats
125 g (4½ oz/⅔ cup) soft brown sugar
30 g (1 oz/½ cup) shredded coconut
1 teaspoon ground cinnamon
80 g (2¾ oz) unsalted butter, melted

Preheat the oven to 180°C (350°F/Gas 4).
Brush a shallow, 2 litre (70 fl oz/8 cup) baking
dish generously with butter.

Peel, core and roughly chop the apples.
Place in a saucepan with the lemon juice and
125 ml (4 fl oz/½ cup) water. Cover and cook
over low heat for 10 minutes, or until the apples
are just tender. Add the caster sugar and gently
stir until dissolved, then set aside to cool slightly.

To make the crumble topping, cut the
bread into 1 cm (½ inch) cubes and place in
a bowl with the oats, brown sugar, coconut and
cinnamon and gently mix together. Pour the
melted butter over and mix gently to combine.

Spoon the apples into the baking dish and
spread the crumble mixture over the top. Bake
for 25–30 minutes, or until the crumble topping
is golden brown and crisp.

Serve warm, with whipped cream or vanilla
ice cream.

Wholemeal (whole-wheat) bread
can also be used in the crumble
topping instead of white bread.
As a serving suggestion, stir 250 ml
(9 fl oz/1 cup) cream into 375 ml
(13 fl oz/1½ cups) thick vanilla
custard and serve with the warm
crumble. For adults, add a spoonful
of brandy to the custard if desired.

Sweet baked ricotta cake with cherries

The cherries can be cooked a day or two in advance and stored in an airtight container in the refrigerator. For the adults, a splash or two of kirsch or Grand Marnier can be added to the cherries after the children have been served — or the adults' portions can be served with a spoonful or two of cream that has been whipped with a little caster (superfine) sugar and some liqueur.

melted butter, for greasing
35 g (1¼ oz/⅓ cup) ground almonds
80 g (2¾ oz/⅓ cup) caster (superfine) sugar
1 kg (2 lb 4 oz/4 cups) firm, fresh ricotta cheese
1 teaspoon natural vanilla extract
½ teaspoon natural almond extract (optional)
finely grated rind of 1 orange
60 ml (2 fl oz/¼ cup) orange juice
4 eggs, lightly beaten
35 g (1¼ oz/¼ cup) plain (all-purpose) flour
125 g (4½ oz/1 cup) slivered almonds

Stewed cherries
80 ml (2½ fl oz/⅓ cup) orange juice
90 g (3¼ oz/⅓ cup) caster (superfine) sugar
1 cinnamon stick
600 g (1 lb 5 oz) fresh or frozen pitted cherries

Put all the ingredients for the stewed cherries in a saucepan. Cover with a lid, then slowly bring to the boil over medium heat. Cook for 8–10 minutes, or until the cherries are tender. Remove from the heat, allow to cool to room temperature, then remove the cinnamon stick and discard.

Meanwhile, preheat the oven to 170°C (325°F/Gas 3). Brush the base and side of a 23 cm (9 inch) springform tin with melted butter, then dust the tin with the ground almonds, turning the tin to coat it evenly. Shake out any excess.

Put the sugar, ricotta, vanilla and almond extracts, orange rind and orange juice in a food processor and blend until smooth, stopping the machine occasionally to scrape down the sides. With the motor running, add the beaten eggs, processing until smooth, then add the flour and process until just combined.

Pour the mixture into the springform tin, smoothing the top even. Sprinkle with the slivered almonds and bake for 40–45 minutes, or until the cake is just firm in the middle. Turn the oven off, open the door slightly and leave the cake to cool completely. Serve at room temperature or chilled, with the stewed cherries spooned over.

Preparation time:
30 minutes

Cooking time:
1 hour

Serves:
2 adults, 3 kids (with leftovers)

Preparation time: 25 minutes
plus 10 minutes cooling

Cooking time:
1 hour 35 minutes

Serves:
2 adults, 3 kids

Jaffa steamed pudding with chocolate sauce

melted butter, for greasing
2 tablespoons marmalade
1 small orange
125 g (4½ oz) unsalted butter, softened
115 g (4 oz/½ cup) caster (superfine) sugar
75 g (2½ oz/½ cup) chopped dark chocolate, melted and cooled
2 eggs
110 g (3¾ oz/¾ cup) self-raising flour
35 g (1¼ oz/¼ cup) plain (all-purpose) flour
30 g (1 oz/¼ cup) unsweetened cocoa powder
60 ml (2 fl oz/¼ cup) milk

Chocolate sauce
1 tablespoon soft brown sugar
125 g (4½ oz/¾ cup) chopped dark chocolate
80 ml (2½ fl oz/⅓ cup) cream

Extras, for adults
Cointreau or brandy, to taste

Lightly brush a 1.25 litre (44 fl oz/5 cup) pudding basin with melted butter. Line the base with a round of baking paper, then spread the marmalade over the base.

Finely grate the orange rind and set aside. Using a sharp knife, remove all the white pith from the orange. Cut the orange into five or six slices widthways, removing any seeds. Overlap the slices around the bottom of the pudding basin and a little up the sides.

Beat the butter, sugar and orange rind using electric beaters until light and fluffy. Add the melted chocolate and beat in well. Add the eggs one at a time, beating well after each addition.

Sift together the flours and cocoa. Stir into the butter mixture in two batches, alternating with the milk. Spoon into the pudding basin and smooth the surface even.

Lay a sheet of foil on a work surface and top with a sheet of baking paper. Make a large pleat in the centre and place over the pudding basin, foil side up. Tie securely around the basin with string. Place on a trivet or an inverted heatproof saucer in a large saucepan. Fill the pan with boiling water to come halfway up the side of the basin. Bring the saucepan to the boil, then cover and cook over medium heat for 1½ hours, adding more water as necessary. Remove the string and foil cover and stand the pudding for 10 minutes to firm slightly.

Put the chocolate sauce ingredients in a small saucepan and stir over low heat for 2–3 minutes, or until melted and glossy.

Turn the pudding out onto a large plate. Cut into wedges and serve with the chocolate sauce.

For the adults, stir some Cointreau or brandy into the chocolate sauce.

Grape jelly with whipped cream and fennel

500 ml (17 fl oz/2 cups) grape juice
3 teaspoons powdered gelatine
55 g (2 oz/¼ cup) caster (superfine)
  sugar, or to taste
150 g (5½ oz) seedless red grapes,
  washed, dried and sliced in half
vanilla ice cream, to serve

Extras, for adults
125 ml (4 fl oz/½ cup) cream, whipped
2½ teaspoons caster (superfine) sugar
¼ teaspoon fennel seeds, crushed

Pour 60 ml (2 fl oz/¼ cup) of the grape juice into a small heatproof bowl or cup and sprinkle the gelatine over the top. Stand for 5 minutes, or until the gelatine has softened, then place the cup in a small saucepan of hot water deep enough to come halfway up the side of the cup. Stand over medium–low heat for 3–4 minutes, or until the gelatine has dissolved, ensuring that the water in the saucepan doesn't boil.

Heat the remaining grape juice and sugar in a small saucepan over low heat, stirring to dissolve the sugar. Pour into a bowl, stir in the gelatine mixture until well combined, then leave to cool to room temperature.

Stir the grape halves into the cooled mixture and divide among four 250 ml (9 fl oz/1 cup) glasses. Refrigerate for 2 hours, or until the jellies have set.

For the kids, serve the jellies with a scoop of vanilla ice cream.

For the adults, whisk the whipped cream and sugar in a bowl until soft peaks form, then dollop over the jellies and sprinkle with the crushed fennel seeds.

Preparation time: 10 minutes
plus 2 hours chilling

Cooking time:
5 minutes

Serves:
2 adults, 2 kids

| ❋ **Preparation time:** 15 minutes | ❋ **Cooking time:** 30 minutes | ❋ **Serves:** 2 adults, 3 kids |

Chocolate brownie ice cream sandwiches

125 g (4½ oz) unsalted butter

250 g (9 oz/1⅔ cups) chopped good-
quality dark chocolate

150 g (5½ oz/⅔ cup) caster (superfine)
sugar

3 eggs, lightly beaten

2 teaspoons natural vanilla extract

100 g (3½ oz/⅔ cup) plain (all-purpose)
flour

30 g (1 oz/¼ cup) unsweetened
cocoa powder

65 g (2¼ oz/½ cup) sultanas (golden
raisins)

5 individually wrapped ice cream slices

2 tablespoons icing (confectioners')
sugar, sifted

Preheat the oven to 170ºC (325ºF/Gas 3). Line a 20 x 30 cm (8 x 12 inch) rectangular tin with baking paper.

Melt the butter in a small saucepan over low heat, then add the chocolate and stir until the chocolate has melted. Remove from the heat, add the sugar and stir well. Leave to cool slightly.

Add the eggs one at a time to the chocolate mixture, mixing well after each addition. Stir in the vanilla.

Sift the flour and cocoa into a bowl, then add the chocolate mixture and sultanas and stir to combine. Pour the mixture into the baking tin, smoothing the top even. Bake for 20–25 minutes, or until a cake tester inserted into the centre comes out clean. Leave the brownies in the tin to cool completely.

To serve, cut the brownies into 6 x 9 cm (2½ x 3½ inch) portions, or into pieces the same size as the ice cream slices, trimming the edges even. Place one brownie on each plate, top with an ice cream slice, then top with another brownie. Dust with the icing sugar and serve.

You can also use chopped nuts or shredded coconut in the brownies instead of the sultanas.

Apricot sponge pudding

3 x 410 g (14½ oz) tins apricot halves
  in natural juice
55 g (2 oz/¼ cup) caster (superfine)
  sugar
125 g (4½ oz/⅔ cup) soft brown sugar
125 g (4½ oz) unsalted butter, softened
2 eggs
1 teaspoon natural vanilla extract
150 g (5½ oz/1 cup) plain (all-purpose)
  flour
2 teaspoons baking powder
60 ml (2 fl oz/¼ cup) milk
custard, to serve

Extras, for adults
2½ tablespoons amaretto (almond-
  flavoured liqueur)

Preheat the oven to 170°C (325°F/Gas 3).

Put the apricots and their juice in a saucepan
with the caster sugar over medium heat. Bring
to the boil, then reduce the heat to medium–low
and simmer for 5 minutes, or until the apricots
have softened.

Reserving the syrup in the pan, spoon the
apricots into a 2 litre (70 fl oz/8 cup) baking
dish (measuring about 14 x 20 x 7 cm/5½ x 8 x
2¾ inches). Place the syrup back over medium
heat and simmer for a further 12–15 minutes, or
until reduced by half. Pour over the apricots.

Beat the brown sugar and butter with electric
beaters until light and fluffy. Add the eggs one at
a time, beating well after each addition. Stir in
the vanilla.

Sift the flour and baking powder together,
then stir into the butter mixture alternately with
the milk. Spoon the batter over the apricots,
spreading it to cover the fruit.

Bake for 30–35 minutes, or until the sponge
is golden and firm to the touch. Serve hot,
with custard.

For the adults, serve the sponge sprinkled with
the amaretto.

Preparation time:
20 minutes

Cooking time:
55 minutes

Serves:
2 adults, 3 kids

✳ **Preparation time:** 20 minutes
plus several hours (or overnight) freezing

✳ **Cooking time:**
5 minutes

✳ **Makes:** 12
(6 of each variety)

Chocolate-dipped ice cream balls

1 litre (35 fl oz/4 cups) vanilla ice cream (*see tip*)
150 g (5½ oz/1 cup) chopped good-quality milk chocolate (*see tip*)
150 g (5½ oz/1 cup) chopped good-quality dark chocolate (*see tip*)
1 tablespoon vegetable oil
3 tablespoons hundreds and thousands
40 g (1½ oz/⅓ cup) chopped pistachio nuts

Line two baking trays with baking paper and freeze until very cold.

Working quickly, scoop six large balls of ice cream onto each chilled baking tray. Insert an ice cream stick or small cocktail toothpick into each ball. Put the trays in the freezer for several hours or overnight, until the ice cream balls are firm.

Melt the milk chocolate and dark chocolate in separate heatproof bowls set over saucepans of simmering water, ensuring the water does not touch the base of the bowls. Stir the chocolate until smooth. Stir half the oil into the milk chocolate and the remainder into the dark chocolate. Cool to room temperature.

Have the toppings prepared as you will need to work quickly. Work with one tray of ice cream balls at a time.

For the kids, with the aid of the attached stick and a spoon, dip six balls in the milk chocolate, using the spoon to coat the balls and letting the excess chocolate drip off. Immediately sprinkle with the hundreds and thousands, then quickly return to the tray and refreeze for 2 hours, or overnight.

For the adults, dip the remaining ice cream balls in the dark chocolate and immediately sprinkle with the chopped pistachios. Quickly return to the tray and refreeze for 2 hours, or overnight.

Use any ice cream flavours for this recipe, although it's best to use a firmer ice cream rather than a very creamy variety as it is easier to work with. It is also important to use good-quality chocolate as cheaper brands may not adhere well to the ice cream. Try using a good-quality white chocolate for coating the balls, or decorating with different toppings such as sprinkles, lightly toasted flaked almonds or flaked chocolate.

Golden syrup coconut dumplings with lime custard

For a stronger coconut flavour, add a few drops of coconut essence to the coconut milk when making the dumplings.

200 g (7 oz/1⅓ cups) plain (all-purpose) flour
45 g (1½ oz/½ cup) desiccated coconut
45 g (1½ oz) unsalted butter, chopped
55 g (2 oz/¼ cup) caster (superfine) sugar
125–170 ml (4–5½ fl oz/½–⅔ cup) coconut milk
whipped cream or vanilla ice cream, to serve

Lime custard, for the adults
500 ml (17 fl oz/2 cups) custard
½ teaspoon finely grated lime rind
1 tablespoon lime juice

Syrup
40 g (1½ oz) unsalted butter, chopped
155 g (5½ oz/¾ cup) soft brown sugar
235 g (8½ oz/⅔ cup) golden syrup or dark corn syrup

Put all the lime custard ingredients in a bowl and mix well. Cover with plastic wrap and refrigerate until needed.

Mix the flour and coconut in a large bowl with a large pinch of salt. Rub in the butter with your fingertips until the mixture resembles coarse breadcrumbs. Stir in the sugar, then make a well in the centre. Using a flat-bladed knife, mix in enough coconut milk to make a soft dough.

To make the syrup, put the butter, sugar, golden syrup and 435 ml (15¼ fl oz/1¾ cups) water in a large (23 cm/9 inch) frying pan. Stir over medium heat until the butter has melted and the sugar has dissolved. Bring to the boil, then reduce the heat to a low simmer. Add heaped teaspoons of the coconut mixture to the hot syrup, in a single layer.

Cover and cook over very low heat for 15–20 minutes, or until the dumplings are cooked through. Leave to cool slightly, then carefully turn the dumplings over and spoon onto serving plates.

For the kids, serve with whipped cream or vanilla ice cream.

For the adults, serve with the lime custard.

Preparation time:	Cooking time:	Serves:
35 minutes	25 minutes	2 adults, 3 kids

Preparation time:
15 minutes

Cooking time:
5 minutes

Serves:
2 adults, 2 kids

Caramel banana splits

8 frozen waffles (each about 6 x 9 cm/
  2½ x 3½ inches), thawed
20 g (¾ oz) unsalted butter
200 ml (7 fl oz) tinned caramel sauce
  (or see our recipe on page 178)
4 firm but ripe bananas
1½ tablespoons lemon juice, or to taste
4 scoops of vanilla ice cream
2 tablespoons grated milk chocolate

Extras, for adults
2 tablespoons chopped roasted
  macadamia nuts
rum or brandy, to taste

Preheat the grill (broiler) to medium.

Using a large serrated knife, cut the waffles in half widthways and place on a baking tray. Grill (broil) for 2 minutes on each side, or until golden and crisp.

Meanwhile, melt the butter in a small saucepan. Add the caramel sauce and whisk over low heat until smooth, then allow to cool.

Cut the bananas into thick slices on the diagonal and sprinkle with the lemon juice. Put two waffles decoratively at an angle in each serving bowl. Arrange the banana slices in a stack next to the waffles and add a scoop of ice cream.

For the kids, spoon half the caramel sauce over, sprinkle with the grated chocolate and serve.

For the adults, stir the rum or brandy into the remaining caramel sauce, drizzle over the bananas and ice cream and serve scattered with the nuts.

Rocky road ice cream terrine

180 g (6 oz/¾ cup) chopped glacé
cherries
180 g (6 oz/2 cups) marshmallows,
chopped
65 g (2¼ oz/¾ cup) desiccated coconut
100 g (3½ oz) chocolate wafer biscuits,
chopped
150 g (5½ oz/1 cup) chopped milk
chocolate
2 litres (70 fl oz/8 cups) vanilla
ice cream
60 ml (2 fl oz/¼ cup) chocolate syrup

Line a 3 litre (104 fl oz/12 cup) loaf (bar) tin with baking paper, allowing a 5 cm (2 inch) overhang at both ends. Place in the freezer for 30 minutes.

Put the cherries, marshmallows, coconut and wafers in a large bowl and gently mix together.

Melt the chocolate in a heatproof bowl over a saucepan half-filled with simmering water, ensuring the base of the bowl doesn't touch the water. Stir the melted chocolate through the marshmallow mixture, mixing well to coat the ingredients with the chocolate. Allow to cool to room temperature.

Meanwhile, remove the ice cream from the freezer for 10 minutes, or until softened slightly. Fold the marshmallow mixture into the softened ice cream and stir to combine well.

Spoon the ice cream into the loaf tin, smoothing the top even, then freeze for 3 hours or overnight, until firm.

To serve, stand the ice cream in the loaf tin at room temperature for 5 minutes to soften slightly before turning out onto a plate. Cut into slices 2 cm (¾ inch) thick and drizzle with chocolate syrup.

Preparation time: 15 minutes
plus 3 hours (or overnight) freezing

Cooking time:
5 minutes

Serves: 2 adults,
3 kids (with leftovers)

163   DINNER WITH KIDS

Preparation time: 15 minutes
plus several hours (or overnight) cooling

Cooking time:
50 minutes

Makes:
1 loaf

Date, raisin and pecan loaf

240 g (8½ oz/1½ cups) chopped
  pitted dates
125 g (4½ oz/1 cup) raisins
30 g (1 oz) unsalted butter, chopped
60 g (2¼ oz/⅓ cup) soft brown sugar
300 g (10½ oz/2 cups) self-raising flour
1 teaspoon mixed spice (pumpkin
  pie spice)
1 egg, lightly beaten
1 tablespoon vegetable oil
1 tablespoon golden syrup or dark
  corn syrup
60 ml (2 fl oz/¼ cup) milk
100 g (3½ oz/1 cup) pecans, roughly
  chopped

Extras, for kids
1 banana, sliced lengthways, to serve
vanilla ice cream, to serve
tinned caramel sauce, for drizzling
  (or see our recipe on page 178)

Extras, for adults
assorted cheeses, to serve
grapes, to serve
quince or guava paste, to serve
  (optional)

Preheat the oven to 160°C (315°F/Gas 2–3).
Lightly grease a 1.5 litre (52 fl oz/6 cup) loaf
(bar) tin (measuring about 10.5 x 21 cm/4 x
8¼ inches) and line the base with baking paper.

Put the dates, raisins, butter and sugar in a
large bowl. Pour 150 ml (5 fl oz) boiling water
over, stirring to melt the butter and to dissolve
the sugar. Leave to stand for 5 minutes for the
fruit to absorb some of the liquid.

Sift the flour and mixed spice into a large
bowl. In a small bowl, whisk together the egg, oil,
golden syrup and milk until well combined, then
pour into the flour mixture, stirring until a smooth
batter forms. Stir the fruit mixture and pecans
through, then pour into the loaf tin, smoothing
the surface even.

Bake for 50 minutes, or until a cake tester
inserted in the centre of the loaf comes out
clean. Leave in the tin to cool for 10 minutes,
before turning out onto a wire rack to cool
completely. Wrap the loaf in plastic wrap and
leave for several hours or overnight before cutting
into thin slices.

For the kids, serve with banana slices and a scoop
of ice cream, drizzled with caramel sauce.

For the adults, serve with a cheese platter, grapes,
and quince or guava paste if desired.

Leave out the nuts if these are not
suitable for your kids. Otherwise you
could replace the pecans with other
nuts such as walnuts or macadamias.
As another variation you could
replace some or all of the dates with
chopped dried figs, and the raisins
with chopped dried apricots. You can
also serve this loaf freshly baked, cut
into thicker slices and spread with
butter. Any leftover loaf can be frozen.

Milk and honey jellies with sherry jelly

500 ml (17 fl oz/2 cups) milk
125 ml (4 fl oz/½ cup) cream
1 cinnamon stick
1 teaspoon natural vanilla extract
115 g (4 oz/⅓ cup) honey
3½ teaspoons powdered gelatine
whipped cream, to serve
grated chocolate, to serve

Sherry jelly, for adults
125 ml (4 fl oz/½ cup) sweet sherry
  or marsala
½ teaspoon powdered gelatine

Put the milk, cream, cinnamon, vanilla and honey in a saucepan and warm over medium–low heat, stirring occasionally to dissolve the honey. Remove from the heat just as the mixture comes to a simmer. Cover with a lid and leave to stand for 30 minutes for the flavours to infuse, stirring occasionally to prevent a skin forming.

Meanwhile, pour 2 tablespoons cold water into a small heatproof glass or cup and sprinkle the gelatine over the top. Leave to stand for 5 minutes, or until the gelatine has softened, then place the glasses in a small saucepan of hot water deep enough to come halfway up the side of the glass. Stand over medium–low heat for 3–4 minutes, or until the gelatine has dissolved, ensuring the water in the saucepan doesn't boil.

Remove the cinnamon stick from the milk, then stir in the gelatine mixture. Leave to cool to room temperature, then stir again to disperse the cream. Pour the mixture into four 250 ml (9 fl oz/ 1 cup) glasses, then cover and refrigerate for 3 hours, or until the jellies have set.

For the adults, top the milk jellies with a layer of sherry jelly. Pour 1 tablespoon of the sherry into a small heatproof cup and sprinkle with the gelatine. Leave for 5 minutes, or until the gelatine has softened, then place the cup in a small saucepan of hot water deep enough to come halfway up the side of the cup. Stand over medium–low heat for 3–4 minutes, or until the gelatine has dissolved, ensuring the water in the pan doesn't boil. Pour into a bowl, stir in the remaining sherry and cool to room temperature. Pour the mixture over two of the milk jellies and refrigerate for 3 hours, or until set.

To serve, top the jellies with a dollop of whipped cream and sprinkle with grated chocolate.

Preparation time: 15 minutes
plus 30 minutes standing and 6 hours chilling

Cooking time:
10 minutes

Serves:
2 adults, 2 kids

Preparation time:
5 minutes

Cooking time:
10–15 minutes

Serves:
2 adults, 3 kids

Banana fritters

1 litre (35 fl oz/4 cups) vegetable oil,
  for deep-frying
375 g (13 oz/2½ cups) self-raising flour
½ teaspoon bicarbonate of soda
  (baking soda)
4 firm but ripe bananas
5 scoops of vanilla ice cream
warmed maple or golden syrup,
  to serve

Extras, for adults
2 tablespoons roughly chopped
  toasted pecans

Pour the oil into a saucepan and place over medium heat. Heat the oil to 180°C (350°F), or until a cube of bread dropped into the oil turns golden in 15 seconds.

Set aside 75 g (2½ oz/½ cup) of the flour in a bowl. Sift the remaining flour and the bicarbonate of soda into a large bowl, then add 435 ml (15¼ fl oz/1¾ cups) water and whisk to a smooth batter.

Peel the bananas and cut them in half widthways, then cut each piece in half lengthways. Working in batches, dust each banana piece in the flour, shaking off the excess, then dip them into the batter, draining off the excess.

Deep-fry the fritters in batches for 5–6 minutes each time, or until the batter is golden and crisp. Briefly drain on paper towels and serve hot with a scoop of ice cream, drizzled with maple syrup.

For the adults, sprinkle the fritters with the pecans.

Apple and peach turnovers

40 g (1½ oz/⅓ cup) dried peaches,
  finely chopped
25 g (1 oz) unsalted butter
2 tablespoons soft brown sugar
3 granny smith apples, peeled,
  cored and finely chopped
1 teaspoon ground cinnamon
4 sheets of frozen shortcrust pastry,
  thawed
1 egg, lightly beaten
sifted icing (confectioners') sugar,
  for dusting
thick (double/heavy) cream, to serve

Extras, for adults
2 tablespoons lightly toasted blanched
  almonds, finely chopped
1 tablespoon sweet sherry
2 tablespoons soft brown sugar
125 ml (4 fl oz/½ cup) thick (double/heavy)
  cream

Preheat the oven to 180°C (350°F/Gas 4).
Line a baking tray with baking paper.

Put the dried peaches in a small bowl,
pour 250 ml (9 fl oz/1 cup) boiling water over
and leave to soak for 10 minutes.

Put the butter and sugar in a frying pan and
stir over medium heat until the butter melts.
Add the apple and cinnamon and cook, stirring
frequently, for 3–4 minutes, or until the apple
has softened. Drain the soaked peaches, stir
them through the apple mixture and set
aside to cool.

Lay the pastry sheets on a work surface and
cut out eight circles using a 12 cm (4½ inch)
cutter. Place 2 tablespoons of the apple mixture
in the middle of each circle. Lightly brush the
edge of each pastry with beaten egg, then fold
each one over to form a semi-circle, firmly
pressing the edges to seal.

Place the turnovers on the baking tray and
brush the tops with the remaining egg. Bake
for 25–30 minutes, or until the pastry is golden
brown. Remove from the oven and allow to cool
slightly before dusting with icing sugar.

For the kids, serve the turnovers with a dollop
of cream.

For the adults, combine the almonds, sherry,
sugar and cream in a small bowl and serve with
the warm turnovers.

Preparation time: 10 minutes
plus 10 minutes soaking

Cooking time:
35 minutes

Makes: 8

Preparation time: 20 minutes
plus about 3 hours chilling

Cooking time:
10 minutes

Serves:
2 adults, 2 kids

White chocolate mousse with strawberries

180 g (6 oz/1⅓ cups) chopped
  good-quality white chocolate
300 ml (10½ fl oz) cream
1 teaspoon powdered gelatine
3 eggs, separated
250 g (9 oz) strawberries, hulled
  and sliced
sifted icing (confectioners') sugar,
  for dusting

Extras, for adults
1½ tablespoons Cointreau or other
  orange-flavoured liqueur
1 tablespoon sifted icing (confectioners')
  sugar
1 small handful of mint leaves, torn

Put the chocolate and cream in a heatproof bowl set over a saucepan of simmering water, ensuring the water does not touch the base of the bowl. Stir until the chocolate has melted and the mixture is smooth, then set aside to cool.

Pour 1 tablespoon water into a small heatproof cup and sprinkle the gelatine over the top. Leave to stand for 5 minutes, or until the gelatine has softened, then place the cup in a small saucepan of hot water deep enough to come halfway up the side of the cup. Stand over medium–low heat for 3–4 minutes, or until the gelatine has dissolved, ensuring the water in the saucepan doesn't boil. Allow to cool slightly, then stir into the chocolate mixture along with the egg yolks. Refrigerate for 20 minutes, or until thickened slightly.

Using electric beaters, whisk the egg whites in a dry, clean bowl until firm peaks form. Fold the egg white into the chocolate mixture until evenly combined. Divide among four 250 ml (9 fl oz/1 cup) serving glasses, then cover and refrigerate for 3 hours, or until set.

Half an hour before serving, macerate some strawberries for the adults. Toss half the strawberries in a small bowl with the liqueur and icing sugar, then cover and leave to stand for 30 minutes.

For the kids, serve the mousse topped with the plain strawberries and a dusting of icing sugar.

For the adults, stir the mint leaves through the macerated strawberries and spoon over the mousse.

Brown sugar rice pudding with prune compote

The rice can be served warm or at room temperature and can be made up to 3 days in advance; store in an airtight container in the refrigerator. This recipe can easily be doubled and can also be served with other stewed fruits such as apples, peaches, apricots, rhubarb or quince.

1 litre (35 fl oz/4 cups) milk
75 g (2½ oz/⅓ cup) short-grain white rice
125 g (4½ oz/⅔ cup) soft brown sugar
½ vanilla bean, or 1 teaspoon natural vanilla extract
whipped cream, to serve (optional)
ground cinnamon, to serve (optional)

Prune compote
300 g (10½ oz/1⅓ cups) pitted prunes
250 ml (9 fl oz/1 cup) orange juice
45 g (1½ oz/¼ cup) soft brown sugar

Extras, for adults
2 tablespoons brandy or whisky, or to taste

Put the prune compote ingredients in a small saucepan and bring to a gentle simmer. Cook, uncovered, over medium–low heat for 10 minutes, or until the prunes are very soft and the liquid has reduced a little. Remove from the heat and allow to cool to room temperature, then cover and refrigerate.

Meanwhile, put the milk, rice and sugar in a saucepan. If using the vanilla bean, split it in half lengthways using a small sharp knife, then scrape the seeds into the milk mixture. Add the bean (or vanilla extract, if using) to the milk and slowly bring to a simmer, stirring occasionally. Reduce the heat to very low and cook, stirring occasionally, for 1 hour 10 minutes, or until the mixture is thickened and creamy — take care it doesn't stick to the pan and burn. Discard the vanilla bean and divide the rice among two bowls (the rice will thicken as it cools).

Drain half the prunes well, chop finely, then stir into one of the rice bowls. Cover both bowls and refrigerate until chilled.

For the kids, divide the rice containing the chopped prunes among serving glasses or bowls.

For the adults, stir the brandy or whisky through the remaining prune compote and serve over the plain rice.

Serve each bowl with a spoonful of whipped cream and a sprinkling of cinnamon, if using.

Preparation time: 15 minutes
plus chilling

Cooking time:
1 hour 20 minutes

Serves:
2 adults, 3 kids

Preparation time: 10 minutes
plus 30 minutes resting

Cooking time:
25 minutes

Makes: 12

Lemon crepes

225 g (8 oz/1½ cups) plain
   (all-purpose) flour
2 tablespoons caster (superfine) sugar
3 eggs
500 ml (17 fl oz/2 cups) milk
20 g (¾ oz) melted butter, cooled,
   plus extra butter, for pan-frying

Extras, for kids
sifted icing (confectioners') sugar,
   to serve
lemon wedges, to serve

Extras, for adults
115 g (4 oz/½ cup) ready-made
   lemon curd (lemon butter)
2 tablespoons thick (double/heavy)
   cream
fresh raspberries, to serve

Sift the flour and a pinch of salt into a bowl, then stir in the sugar and make a well in the centre.

Whisk the eggs in a small bowl with the milk and melted butter. Pour into the flour mixture and whisk until smooth. Strain the batter into a pouring jug to eliminate any lumps, then cover with plastic wrap and refrigerate for 30 minutes.

Heat a 22 cm (8½ inch) non-stick frying pan over medium heat. Lightly brush with melted butter, then pour 60 ml (2 fl oz/¼ cup) of the batter into the pan, swirling to coat the pan. Cook for 1 minute, or until the edges are golden, then turn the crepe over and cook for a further minute, or until light golden underneath. Transfer to a warm plate and cover with a paper towel. Repeat with the remaining batter to make 12 crepes, adding a little more butter to the pan as necessary.

For the kids, fold the crepes into quarters and serve sprinkled with a little icing sugar and a squeeze of lemon juice.

For the adults, mix the lemon curd and cream together and spoon into the crepes before folding. Serve scattered with raspberries.

You may need to cook a few crepes before you get the crepe thickness and pan temperature just right — it's quite normal for the first few crepes to be less than perfect. There's plenty of batter in this recipe to allow for any mishaps and produce 12 good crepes.

Pear, caramel and pecan sundaes

Instead of serving children the nuts, you can use small, crushed meringues. The adults might like a small splash of dark rum stirred into their caramel sauce before assembling their sundaes.

425 g (15 oz) tin pear halves, drained and roughly chopped
8 small scoops of vanilla ice cream (about 500 ml/17 fl oz/2 cups)

Crunchy cinnamon pecans
1 small egg white
55 g (2 oz/¼ cup) caster (superfine) sugar
½ teaspoon ground cinnamon
100 g (3½ oz/1 cup) pecans

Caramel sauce
125 ml (4 fl oz/½ cup) cream
140 g (5 oz/¾ cup) soft brown sugar
90 g (3¼ oz) unsalted butter, chopped

Preheat the oven to 180°C (350°F/Gas 4). Line a baking tray with baking paper.

To make the crunchy cinnamon pecans, beat the egg white in a bowl using electric beaters until soft peaks form. Fold in the sugar, cinnamon and pecans, then spread the pecans in a single layer on the baking tray. Bake for 10–15 minutes, or until the pecan coating is crisp and dry, turning once. Remove from the oven and allow to cool completely.

Meanwhile, make the caramel sauce. Put the cream, sugar and butter in a small saucepan and stir over medium heat until the butter has melted and the sugar has dissolved. Bring to the boil, then reduce the heat to medium–low and simmer for 5 minutes, or until the sauce has thickened slightly. Remove from the heat and allow to cool completely.

Divide the pears among six 300 ml (10½ fl oz) serving glasses, then top each with a scoop of ice cream. Drizzle with about 1 tablespoon of the caramel sauce and add a few of the pecans. Add another scoop of ice cream, drizzle with the remaining caramel sauce, top with the remaining pecans and serve.

Preparation time: 30 minutes
plus 6 hours draining and 6–8 hours
(or overnight) freezing

Cooking time: nil

Makes: 10

Yoghurt, coconut and apricot ice cream sticks

1 kg (2 lb 4 oz/4 cups) Greek-style
  yoghurt
30 g (1 oz/⅓ cup) flaked almonds,
  lightly toasted
40 g (1½ oz/⅓ cup) sultanas (golden
  raisins)
25 g (1 oz/¼ cup) desiccated coconut
45 g (1½ oz/¼ cup) dried apricots,
  chopped
1 teaspoon natural vanilla extract
175 g (6 oz/½ cup) honey
2 tablespoons sesame seeds,
  lightly toasted

Line a large sieve or colander with muslin (cheesecloth), then spoon the yoghurt into the sieve. Stand the sieve over a large bowl. Refrigerate for 6 hours or overnight, or until the yoghurt is well drained and thickened.

Remove the yoghurt to a large bowl. In a food processor, very finely chop the almonds, sultanas, coconut and apricot, then add to the yoghurt with the remaining ingredients and stir to combine well.

Divide the mixture among ten 120 ml (3¾ fl oz) ice cream moulds, then insert an ice cream stick into the middle of each one. Freeze for 6–8 hours or overnight, until frozen solid.

To serve, dip the moulds briefly in a bowl of hot water to loosen the frozen yoghurts. Serve immediately.

The yoghurt ice cream sticks can be frozen for up to 8 days.

Rich chocolate puddings

Use milk chocolate if you prefer a milder chocolate flavour. For a jaffa flavour, stir in 1½ teaspoons finely grated orange rind, or ½ teaspoon ground cinnamon for a hint of spice. For adults, stir a little orange- or coffee-flavoured liqueur into the whipped cream before topping.

115 g (4 oz/½ cup) caster (superfine) sugar
750 ml (26 fl oz/3 cups) milk
30 g (1 oz/¼ cup) unsweetened cocoa powder
30 g (1 oz/¼ cup) cornflour (cornstarch)
1 egg, plus 1 egg yolk
150 g (5½ oz/1 cup) chopped dark chocolate (*see tip*)
1 teaspoon natural vanilla extract
whipped cream, to serve
grated chocolate, to serve

Put the sugar in a saucepan with 625 ml (21½ fl oz/2½ cups) of the milk. Stir to dissolve the sugar and slowly bring the milk to a simmer over medium heat.

Meanwhile, sift the cocoa and cornflour into a large bowl. Add the remaining milk and whisk until a smooth paste forms.

Whisking continuously, add the hot milk to the cocoa mixture, whisking to combine well. Return the mixture to the saucepan, reserving the bowl, and whisk constantly over medium heat for 3 minutes, or until the mixture boils and thickens. Remove from the heat.

In the reserved bowl, combine the egg and egg yolk. Whisking continuously, add the hot chocolate mixture in a steady stream, whisking until smooth. Add the chopped chocolate and stir until the chocolate has melted and the mixture is smooth.

Allow to cool to room temperature, stirring occasionally to prevent a skin forming, then divide among five 250 ml (9 fl oz/1 cup) serving glasses or cups. Cover with plastic wrap and refrigerate for several hours, or until chilled.

Serve dolloped with whipped cream and sprinkled with grated chocolate.

Preparation time: 15 minutes
plus 2–3 hours chilling

Cooking time:
10 minutes

Serves:
2 adults, 3 kids

Preparation time:
25 minutes

Cooking time:
30 minutes

Serves:
2 adults, 3 kids

Tropical Eton mess

2 egg whites
115 g (4 oz/½ cup) caster (superfine)
  sugar
500 ml (17 fl oz/2 cups) cream
440 g (15½ oz) tin crushed pineapple,
  drained
170 g (5¾ oz) tin passionfruit pulp

Preheat the oven to 140°C (275°F/Gas 1).
Line two baking trays with baking paper.

Using electric beaters, whisk the egg whites
in a dry, clean bowl until stiff peaks form. Add
the sugar 1 tablespoon at a time, beating well
after each addition. Beat until the mixture is
thick and glossy and the sugar has dissolved
— this should take about 10 minutes.

Spoon rounded dessertspoonfuls of the
mixture onto the baking trays, then bake for
25–30 minutes, or until the meringues are
pale and dry. Turn the oven off and leave the
meringues in the oven for 20 minutes to cool
completely, leaving the door ajar.

Pour the cream into a large bowl and whip
until soft peaks form, using electric beaters.

Break each meringue into 2.5 cm (1 inch)
chunks and place in a large bowl. Spoon the
crushed pineapple over, then fold in the whipped
cream. Drizzle with two-thirds of the passionfruit
pulp and fold gently to create a swirling effect.

Spoon the mixture into serving bowls, glasses
or cups. Drizzle with the remaining passionfruit
pulp and serve.

Watermelon, cranberry and lime granita

For this amount of juice you'll need a 2.25 kg (5 lb) piece of seedless watermelon. To make the juice, either push the watermelon flesh through a juicer, or blend it in a food processor and then pass it through a sieve.

230 g (8 oz/1 cup) caster (superfine) sugar
125 ml (4 fl oz/½ cup) cranberry juice
750 ml (26 fl oz/3 cups) fresh watermelon juice (*see tip*)
60 ml (2 fl oz/¼ cup) lime juice

Extras, for adults
60 ml (2 fl oz/¼ cup) vanilla vodka

Place a 2 litre (70 fl oz/8 cup) metal baking tin (or one measuring about 20 x 30 x 4 cm/ 8 x 12 x 1½ inches) in the freezer to chill.

Put the sugar in a saucepan with 375 ml (13 fl oz/1½ cups) water. Place over low heat, stirring to dissolve the sugar. Add the cranberry juice, increase the heat to medium–high and bring to the boil. Reduce the heat to low and simmer for 5 minutes. Remove from the heat and leave to cool.

Stir in the watermelon juice and lime juice, then pour into the baking tin and freeze for 2 hours. Remove from the freezer and stir the mixture with a metal fork to break up the ice crystals, then freeze for another hour, or until firm.

Before serving, remove the granita from the freezer for 10 minutes to soften slightly. Using a fork, flake the granita into large crystals. Quickly spoon into serving bowls or cups and serve.

For the adults, serve drizzled with the vodka.

Preparation time: 10 minutes
plus 3 hours freezing

Cooking time:
7 minutes

Serves:
2 adults, 3 kids

INDEX

Published in 2010 by Murdoch Books Pty Limited

Murdoch Books Australia
Pier 8/9
23 Hickson Road
Millers Point NSW 2000
Phone: +61 (0) 2 8220 2000
Fax: +61 (0) 2 8220 2558
www.murdochbooks.com.au

Murdoch Books UK Limited
Erico House, 6th Floor
93–99 Upper Richmond Road
Putney, London SW15 2TG
Phone: +44 (0) 20 8785 5995
Fax: +44 (0) 20 8785 5985
www.murdochbooks.co.uk

Publishing director: Kay Scarlett
Project editor: Kristin Buesing
Copy editor: Katri Hilden
Food editor: Leanne Kitchen
Cover concept: Yolande Gray
Design concept: Emilia Toia
Photographer: Stuart Scott
Stylist: Sarah O'Brien
Food preparation: Grace Campbell
Recipes developed by Peta Dent, Michelle Earl, Heidi Flett, Fiona Hammond, Vicky Harris, Leanne Kitchen, Kathy Knudsen, Barbara Lowery, Kim Meredith, Wendy Quisumbing, Angela Tregonning and the Murdoch Books test kitchen.

National Library of Australia Cataloguing-in-Publication Data
Title: Dinner with kids.
ISBN: 9781741964424 (pbk.)
Series: My Kitchen series.
Notes: Includes index.
Subjects: Dinners and dining. Cookery.
Dewey Number: 641.54
A catalogue record for this book is available from the British Library.

PRINTED IN CHINA.

IMPORTANT: Those who might be at risk from the effects of salmonella poisoning (the elderly, pregnant women, young children and those suffering from immune deficiency diseases) should consult their doctor with any concerns about eating raw eggs.

OVEN GUIDE: You may find cooking times vary depending on the oven you are using. For fan-forced ovens, as a general rule, set the oven temperature to 20°C (35°F) lower than indicated in the recipe.

The **My Kitchen** series is packed with sensational flavours, simple methods and vibrant photographs. What's more, these easy, inexpensive and well-tested recipes use only commonly available ingredients and fresh seasonal produce. And because cooking should be a joy, there's a little bit of magic in them too!

Dinner with Kids takes the frazzle out of mealtimes with a great collection of dinners and desserts the whole family will enjoy. Some are versatile enough to appeal to young and old; others build upon a basic child-friendly recipe to which simple extras are added to delight the adults. The end result? A big saving of time and labour for you – and one big happy family at the dinner table!

£12.99

ISBN 978-1741964424

9 781741 964424

MURDOCH BOOKS